Poems by Adolescents and Adults

A Thematic Collection for Middle School and High School

Edited by

JAMES BREWBAKER
Columbus State University
Columbus, Georgia

DAWNELLE J. HYLAND
Chewning Middle School
Durham, North Carolina

National Council of Teachers of English
1111 W. Kenyon Road, Urbana, Illinois 61801-1096

Staff Editor: Tom Tiller
Interior Design: Jenny Jensen Greenleaf
Cover Design: Pat Mayer

NCTE Stock Number: 35633-3050

It is the policy of NCTE in its journals and other publications to provide a forum for the open discussion of ideas concerning the content and the teaching of English and the language arts. Publicity accorded to any particular point of view does not imply endorsement by the Executive Committee, the Board of Directors, or the membership at large, except in announcements of policy, where such endorsement is clearly specified.

Library of Congress Cataloging-in-Publication Data

Poems by adolescents and adults : a thematic collection for middle school and high school / edited by James Brewbaker [and] Dawnelle J. Hyland.
    p. cm.
Includes bibliographical references.
ISBN 0-8141-3563-3 (pbk.)
   1. Young adult poetry, American 2. Youths' writings, American.
I. Brewbaker, James, 1930– II. Hyland, Dawnelle, J., 1974–

PS586.3 .P637 2002
811'.60809283—dc21

                                         2001044527

CONTENTS

Contents

Contents

Contents

II Close to Home: Classmates, Friends, and Others

Contents

Contents

Contents

Contents

Contents

PERMISSIONS

Grateful acknowledgment is made to the following individuals and publishers for granting permission to reprint material in this book. All student poems published here are used with the permission of both the student poets and their parents; written permissions were secured when the poems were submitted.

Ackerman, Diane: "Pumping Iron," from *Jaguar of Sweet Laughter: New and Selected Poems* by Diane Ackerman (New York: Random House, 1991).

Aguero, Kathleen: "Beating Up Billy Murphy in Fifth Grade," from *The Real Weather* by Aguero Kathleen (Brooklyn: Hanging Loose Press, 1987). Copyright 1987 by Kathleen Aguero. Reprinted by permission of Hanging Loose Press.

Appelt, Kathi: "Who Would've Thought," "That Kiss," and "Keeping His Head," from *Just People and Other Poems for Young Readers & Paper/Pen/Poem: A Young Writer's Way to Begin* (Houston: Absey & Co., 1997).

Balaban, Camille: "a morning like this," from *English Journal* (January 1992). Copyright by the National Council of Teachers of English.

Ball, Joseph H.: "Jenny Says," from *English Journal* (September 1992). Copyright by the National Council of Teachers of English.

Bos, Valerie Voter: "The Dancer," from *Mindscapes: Georgia Student Writing 1990*, Volume IV, edited by Ruby Werts and published by the Georgia Council of Teachers of English (1990, Athens). Reprinted by permission of Valerie Voter Bos.

Brewbaker, James: "Graveyard beside Whitesville Road," from *Flint River Review* 4 (1997). Copyright 1997 by James Brewbaker.

Burk, David: "Outing," from *English Journal* (March 1992). Copyright by the National Council of Teachers of English.

Butson, B. C.: "Girl in the Doorway," from *English Journal* (September 1993). Copyright by the National Council of Teachers of English.

Christensen, Faye D.: "Shadowed Thoughts," from *English Journal* (January 1991). Copyright by the National Council of Teachers of English.

ACKNOWLEDGMENTS

We are grateful to the hundreds of men and women who supported the development of this book. At or near the top of the list of those we thank here are members of the Assembly on Literature for Adolescents of NCTE (ALAN) Research Foundation, which, in 1997, awarded us a generous grant that launched our work. Before we submitted our proposal, ALAN Executive Secretary Ted Hipple advised us on the best approach to take on budget matters and the like. We like to think that, at its best, our work reflects Ted's thinking. Similarly, we value the sensible advice provided by Alan Olds and members of the Advisory Committee of NCTE's Program to Recognize Excellence in Student Literary Magazines when we met with them in Detroit at the 1997 NCTE Annual Convention.

Equally vital to the project early in its development were *English Journal* editor Leila Christenbury and *ALAN Review* co-editors Bob Small and Patricia Kelly. By setting aside precious space in these journals in early 1998 for our call for submissions, Leila, Bob, and Pat guaranteed that English teachers from Vancouver to Key West would be informed about this unique opportunity for their students to publish their best poems. Beyond this national publicity, we know that editors of affiliate journals in many states and communities helped promote participation in the preparation of *Poems by Adolescents and Adults*. We wrote letters to nearly two hundred affiliate officers and editors about our work; many of them passed the word along to their members. The result of their support was our receipt of 1,637 poetry submissions from 835 young people, a number far in excess of our most optimistic expectations.

We cannot recognize by name more than a small percentage of the many teachers who made the extra effort necessary to inform their students about the project; to guide them in polishing one, two, or three poems to the point that they were ready to send them cross-country (or cross-state); to make certain that permissions-to-publish were in place; and the like. "Appendix D: List of Adolescent Poets' Hometowns, Schools, and Teachers" includes the names of sixty teachers whose students have one or more poems chosen for the book. Something on the order of five or six times that number—at least 250 teachers in all—helped us gather so many worthy poems.

Processing this mass of submissions was challenging. For help, we enlisted teacher acquaintances and graduate students in and around Columbus, Georgia. Tom Perry and Claudia Wells—savvy English teachers at Columbus High School and Hardaway High School—were invaluable early reviewers of poems and acted as a sort of backup system to our own screening process. Kathy Jones, Kurt Morton, and Patricia Davis—preservice teachers—helped organize materials and keep track of ratings. Kathy, in particular, did some vital and valuable legwork in reviewing poetry Web sites and articles useful to teachers of poetry.

Following our initial screening of poems, we needed further help in order to narrow down poems by adolescents to a manageable (and publishable) number. To this end, we asked teachers and teacher educators from seven states (Alabama, California, Florida, Georgia, Michigan, Minnesota, and North Carolina) to have their students—including both preservice teachers and adolescents in grades 7 to 12—identify three poems (out of a packet of nine or ten provided by us) that they would be most, or least, likely to select for an anthology. These professionals and friends— Glen Blalock, Pamela Buchanan, Sissi Carroll, Lynne Culp, Kathleen Dorholt, Catherine Dressel, Mark Faust, Tucker Hearn, Sally Hudson Ross, Mary Ann Tighe—participated enthusiastically in this phase of the project.

More than any others, we thank the ninety-six young poets whose work gives this book its appeal, its personality, its insight into their world. We have corresponded with them on several occasions. We like them. To us they represent much of what is good about young people of this generation, the generation that *Newsweek* columnist Anna Quindlen called "Generation Next." The members of Generation Next give us reason to believe that they will be ready to take on the flawed yet beautiful world we will leave them, ready to find their place, to contribute, to see beauty and point it out to others who may be too busy to notice.

Reference

Quindlen, A. (2000, January 1). Now it's time for Generation Next. *Newsweek, 135,* 112.

PREFACE

We believe you will find that *Poems by Adolescents and Adults: A Thematic Collection for Middle School and High School* is a useful and engaging professional work. In it are 107 poems for classroom use penned by young people in grades 5 to 12, as well as 43 poems written by adults, including both well-known poets, such as Nikki Giovanni, Sandra Cisneros, William Stafford, and Gary Soto, and unfamiliar poets, such as Mary Jenkins, Gene Fehler, or maybe even your next-door neighbor. About half of the poems by adults appeared first in *English Journal (EJ)* during the 1990s. These *EJ* poets are our talented colleagues.

The readership we have in mind for this collection comprises middle-level or high school teachers, teacher educators, and their students—including preservice teachers. We know from a number of trials that adolescents respond favorably to these poems, and we've worked with preservice English teachers as they develop engaging lessons and instructional units based on topics and themes drawn from the volume. The poems are a window into the world of adolescents—how they think, how they use language, what they care about.

A Rich Mix of Poems by Adolescents and Poems by Adults

Because we believe that poems by young people and poems by adults should be read, enjoyed, experienced, and studied alongside one another, that is how they are presented here. You'll find Kathi Appelt's "That Kiss" (from her engaging collection *Just People and Other Poems for Young Readers & Paper/Pen/Poem: A Young Writer's Way to Begin*) alongside Jenny Davis's "First Kiss" and Holley Bailey's "Kiss." Jenny was a senior at Clarkston High School in Clarkston, Michigan, when she wrote "First Kiss," and Holley was an eighth grader at Hayes Middle School in Grand Ledge, Michigan, when she wrote her poem, which contains the powerful closing line "My heart kissed the jagged gate." We were fascinated by the different perspectives that Kathi, Jenny, and Holley brought to the nearly universal experience of "The Kiss"—an adult view, a youthful view, a vivid metaphor. Similar nuggets of varying adult and adolescent perspectives can be found throughout the volume.

Lest we mislead you, we should note the coincidence in the fact that Jenny Davis and Holley Bailey are both from Michigan. In fact, twenty-six states plus British Columbia are represented in *Poems by Adolescents and Adults,* and we chose poems from nearly 1,650 submissions from the United States, Canada, and Okinawa. Though the poems that we (assisted by teachers and their students from across the country) selected are very fine work, they are not "winners" of a contest. We left some fine poems on the cutting-room floor because they did not meet our overall needs for the collection, and we selected some because their fit with a topic or theme seemed almost perfect.

Poets' Explanations

Some of our poets, both adolescents and adults, have provided brief essays explaining why and how they wrote the poems they contributed to this work. These explanations illumine the creative process. English teachers may want to use these explanations in order to help young people better understand how a poet draws on personal experience, or how a literary artist determines a poem's organization, selects words, and senses when a poem is finished. Among the adult poets, explanations by Nikki Giovanni and Birmingham poet Charles Ghigna are especially revealing.

Eleven Themes Keyed to the Needs and Interests of Adolescents

We have clustered the poems by themes that reflect the developmental needs and interests of adolescents. This feature—the fact that the book groups poems into eleven sections, such as "Body, Mind, and Spirit," "Peers," "Gender," and "Individual/Group/ Crowd"—should help teachers in creating thematic units on these and related topics. Some of our themes were in place before we chose poems; others, such as "Choices, Choices, Choices" and "The Future: Goals and Dreams," emerged as we reviewed poems during the summer and fall of 1998. Collectively, the eleven themes range from the relatively commonplace ("School Life" and "Peers") to the relatively obscure ("Masks and the Search for Identity").

Of course, poets don't write to a predetermined theme any more than writers of fiction decide that it's time to throw in a symbol. The fact is that we have categorized each poem based on a connection to one of our chosen themes. But it is also inevitable that there are some poems we might have placed elsewhere, and we encourage readers to consider and/or exploit such possibilities.

Linking Poems to Works of Traditional, Contemporary, and Young Adult Literature

Readers should find the section introductions useful. Here we link themes and poems to works of literature—traditional, contemporary, and young adult (YA). Reflecting our passion for YA literature, we devote most of our attention in these introductions to suggesting works of adolescent fiction and nonfiction that teachers might consider using in thematic units along with poems from this collection. Inasmuch as a grant from ALAN, NCTE's Assembly on Literature for Adolescents, defrayed our expenses for developing the collection, it stands to reason that we hope teachers will use it to bring their students together with good poems and high-quality young adult books.

We have suggested titles with our mind's eye on both middle and high school classrooms. We think the tendency of some school systems to use high-quality young adult books in the lower grades—and to leave them out of the ninth- to twelfth-grade curriculum—is regrettable. Thus, many of the titles we recommend are for high school classrooms. For example, we don't think that

Avi's gripping documentary novel *Nothing But the Truth* is as good a choice for grade 7 or 8 as it is for grade 10 or 11. Somewhat older teens, we believe, may find this novel stylistically simple (though engagingly different), and we insist that there is nothing wrong with that. But they have also experienced enough of the contemporary world to reflect substantively on the ugly outcome that may result when irresponsible media and an amoral bureaucracy converge to deal with what, under normal circumstances, would be a minor infraction of a school rule.

Some of the titles we suggest are well known; novels such as Judy Blume's *Are You There God? It's Me, Margaret* (suggested in "Masks and the Search for Identity"), Robert Cormier's *The Chocolate War* ("School Life" and "Choices, Choices, Choices"), and Katherine Paterson's *Bridge to Terabithia* ("Peers") have been classroom standards for many years. Some, though, are much more recent, including works by Colby Rodowsky (*Lucy Peale* in "Choices Choices Choices"), Sharon Draper (*Tears of a Tiger* in "Peers"), Chris Lynch (*Mick* and other titles from the Blue-Eyed Son series in "Masks and the Search for Identity"), and Karen Hesse (*Phoenix Rising* in "Social Issues"). On balance, we think that the books we recommend are a nice mix of those that teachers are probably already familiar with and those that they may want to put on their personal and classroom reading lists.

Teachers' Resources: Books, Articles, and Web Sites on Using and Teaching Poetry

Poems by Adolescents and Adults is not an activities or strategies book. It does not include questions to pose when discussing poems, follow-up assignments, or advice on how to evaluate student work. Others—many of them teachers, some of them poets—have already supplied these materials abundantly and well in recent books, articles, and online resources.

In three appendixes, therefore, we turn our attention, and yours, we hope, to some of the excellent resources for teachers in search of better ways to introduce adolescents to poetry. "Appendix A: Book Resources for Using and Teaching Poetry" describes recent publications on the subject from NCTE and other publishers we admire, such as Teachers and Writers Collaborative. "Appendix B: Annotated List of Recent *English Journal* and *Voices from the Middle* Articles on Using and Teaching Poetry" details many specific strategies that working teachers have devised to enrich the experiences young people may have with reading, responding to, writing, and performing poems. "Appendix C: Recommended Web Sites on Poetry in the Classroom" is an up-to-date listing of sites that we believe teachers will find helpful as they integrate technology into their teaching.

Getting Personal: Jim and Dawnelle's Reflections and Reminiscences

As we put *Poems by Adolescents and Adults* together, we found ourselves reflecting on our own experiences as adolescents. One of us (Jim) grew up in the fifties, while the other (Dawnelle) was a teenager during the eighties and early nineties. In terms of age, education, gender, and professional experience, we are as different as night and day. We talked about these differences, about how they affected the way we judge a poem or a popular performer, and about how they affected our work together. Before long, our musings led us to write brief reminiscences—a paragraph or two—that we have chosen to include in each section introduction. These reflections aren't a *practical* part of *Poems by Adolescents and Adults*, exactly, but they might stimulate teachers to recall their own adolescence or help sensitize them to the issues, concerns, and experiences their students are living through. We hope so.

America Attacked by Terrorism: Adolescents in a Dangerous, Uncertain World

The obscene events of September 11, 2001, in New York, Washington, and western Pennsylvania changed the world in frightening ways for all Americans—adolescents and adults, students and teachers, men, women, boys, and girls. As we go to press, a nation mourns. Some six thousand human beings are still among the missing at the World Trade Center.

We cannot say what next week, month, or year will bring. What we can affirm is this: we have great faith in the generation of teenagers—twenty-two million strong—who will finish secondary school during the first six or seven years of this century. We marvel at their essential optimism, their ability to deal with new things, to grasp the harsh realities facing their country. We admire their knack for handling lives that seem faster, more complex, more stressful, and, yes, more dangerous than those of their parents and grandparents. We loathe kid bashing, the sort we see in the media and hear out of the mouths of state legislators, people who ought to know better. And we have equally great faith in the part we play as English teachers in guiding Generation Next, a generation that will mature in a dangerous, uncertain world, toward academic competence, personal growth, and a sober yet hopeful understanding of what it means to be human.

Reference

Appelt, K. (1997). *Just people and other poems for young readers & Paper/pen/poem: A young writer's way to begin*. Houston: Absey.

INTRODUCTION

In late 1997, we began working to create a new kind of poetry anthology, one that, because we would build in strong appeal to young people, would be a rich resource for classroom teachers and teacher educators. The product of our labors is this volume of 150 poems—more than two-thirds of them by students in grades 5 through 12, with the remainder by published adult poets as well-known as Nikki Giovanni and William Stafford or as obscure as your next-door neighbor. The 107 poems by adolescents represent 26 states plus British Columbia. The 43 poems by adults include 23 that were published in *English Journal* during the 1990s.

We began *Poems by Adolescents and Adults* with three basic beliefs. First, we believed that poetry by adolescents is an untapped resource for classroom use. Second, we believed that teachers should frequently use or "teach" poems by adolescents and adults alongside one another. Third, we believed that, if we gathered good poems from young people and clustered them thematically with good poems by published adult poets, we could provide a unique resource for both English language arts teachers and teacher educators. By mid-1999, manuscript in hand, our beliefs were affirmed. We had built a collection of poems clustered around eleven themes close to the hearts of young people.[1]

Before detailing how we created *Poems by Adolescents and Adults,* we pause briefly to introduce ourselves. *We* are Jim Brewbaker, a veteran teacher educator from Columbus State University (Georgia), and Dawnelle Hyland, a fourth-year language arts teacher from Chewning Middle School (Durham, North Carolina). We are, in a sense, an odd couple. Despite, or maybe because of, our differences (age, geography, gender, professional roles), we formed a partnership that, out of mutual respect, affected the product of our labors in good ways. Jim, who describes himself as a third-rate, occasionally published poet, has greater experience with reading, evaluating, and—when and if his creative juices flow—writing poetry. He has introduced preservice teachers to the joy and power of using poetry in the classroom for more than twenty years. Dawnelle, working with learning-disabled, inner-city sixth graders who are bused into the outer suburbs, is much closer to the minds and hearts of contemporary adolescents. When she began the anthology project, she, like many teachers early in their careers, wasn't exactly sure what to do with poetry. She knew that poetry in the classroom wasn't or shouldn't be about quatrains and metaphor hunts, but what it ought to be about in her own classroom took shape as she and Jim Brewbaker worked on their anthology project.

Put crassly, Jim knows more about poetry than Dawnelle. Dawnelle, from daily experience, knows more directly the ups and downs of teaching today's young people, and she possesses a keen sense of reality-oriented materials that will capture and hold their attention.[2]

Poetry Collections for Adolescents

It might be argued that poetry is ignored by the adolescent literature community. It might be said, as well, that most publishers don't know what to do with poetry—whether traditional or contemporary, and whether culture-based and chronologically organized, or student-centered. Whatever the case, there are relatively few collections of poems available to secondary English teachers which speak to the issues and topics that concern adolescents most.

Stephen Dunning and colleagues' *Reflections on a Gift of Watermelon Pickle*, in its first and second editions (1966, 1995), was and is an exception to the rule. "The Pickle Book" (this is what Jim's seventh graders called it during his years as a teacher at Ransom School in Coconut Grove, Florida) mixes traditional and contemporary poems and poets, and it utilizes striking black and white photographs to set off poems as works of art, a format sharply in contrast with the practice of cramming as many poems onto a page as possible. This was what major textbook publishers of the 1960s did with poetry, probably to save space.

Watermelon Pickle is organized around themes and topics (for example, poems of observation and poems about travel or far-away places), but its thematic structure is loose and not overtly linked to the special concerns of adolescents as distinct from those of people in general.

There have been other excellent collections of poems for adolescents. Many of these are now out of print. In the 1970s, Richard Peck edited three fine anthologies—*Sounds and Silences: Poetry for Now* (1970), *Mindscapes; Poems for the Real World* (1971), and *Pictures That Storm Inside My Head: Poems for the Inner You* (1976). Dell reissued *Mindscapes* in 1990. Peck's anthologies, in a conventional mass-market paperback format, featured a thematic organization. *Mindscapes* includes "Good Times and Money" and "What Do I Really Look Like" among its eleven themes.

Teachers also should not overlook Paul Janeczko's anthologies of contemporary verse oriented toward adolescents. Two that we particularly like are *Looking for Your Name: A Collection of Contemporary Poems* (1993) and *Wherever Home Begins: 100 Contemporary Poems* (1995). *Looking for Your Name* includes 112 American poems on generally serious themes (including beauty and horror, fragility and tenacity, violence, and war). *Where Home Begins* celebrates small-town America in loosely organized clusters dealing with—among other topics—farms, mines, and other workplaces.

Other recent poetry anthologies for adolescents feature individual well-known poets. Gary Soto's *Neighborhood Odes* (1992) includes poems well selected for younger readers; so does his *A Fire in My Hands: A Book of Poems* (1990). These titles, like others by well-known poets and/or fiction writers—for example, Nikki Giovanni's *My House: Poems* (1974) and *Cotton Candy on a Rainy Day: Poems* (1978), Kathi Appelt's *Just People & Paper/Pen/Poem* (1997), Walter Dean Myers's *Brown Angels: An Album of Pictures and Verse* (1993), and Sharon Draper's *Buttered Bones: Collected Poetry* (1997)—contain numerous poems of genuine appeal to young readers, but they are limited in two ways: first, in featuring the work of a single poet, they lean toward being about that poet and his or her work rather than about life experiences, issues, or themes; second, the themes they do address are embedded rather than highlighted. On a poem-by-poem, book-by-book basis, they are coincidentally linked to adolescent concerns rather than planned that way.

It goes without saying that poets, whether traditionally canonical or contemporary, frequently address youthful concerns and themes. Shakespeare, Keats, Dickinson, Hughes: these and many other artists, well known or obscure, write of young love, of relationships with family and peers, of the need to set goals and to think about the future. More often than not, however, poems by mature poets tend to have an older, sadder-but-wiser, or even nostalgic overlay. "The Road Not Taken" deals with making basic choices in one's life. Frost's speaker says that his or her choice "has made all the difference" (whether for good or bad—or, if one reads the poem as ironic, for neither good nor bad, nor any effect at all). Were a sixteen-year-old to write a poem on the same topic or theme, she or he could not really say what difference, if any, choosing the road less traveled might make in the long run.

Poetry by Adolescents: An Untapped Resource

In virtually every school and classroom, teachers have a largely untapped source of poetry that would be meaningful to adolescent readers. These poems are those written by students in the class, students in other classes, and students whose poems are collected and bound in school literary magazines.

Poems written by adolescents have predictable qualities: they frequently address topics and themes that young people care about; they frequently reflect naive or apparently immature perspectives; they are generally less sophisticated stylistically and linguistically than poems by adults. These qualities are unlikely to appeal to some adults; yet, for the same reasons, they may delight other adolescents. At their best, poems written by young people will differ from those by adults, but the differences—thematic, stylistic, and linguistic—have their own unmistakable charm.

A case in point is Mandy Glover's "Grandma and Me" in our "Generations" section.

Grandma and Me

Your pants are too baggy
I like 'em that way
Your hair is too wild
It's a statement I say

What's the world coming to?
Where did it come from before?
In my day we struggled
Today we struggle more

Kids didn't date until late teens
Kids are having sex before their time
The world is scary out there
I think I'll be just fine

Dawnelle liked Mandy's poem immediately. Jim felt lukewarm about it. Dawnelle responded to the engaging, alternating voices of Grandma on the one hand and "me" on the other. Jim thought the intergenerational conflict was pretty obvious, and the words of the two speakers equally so. He bristled a bit at the colloquial title (Why not "Grandma and I" for Pete's sake?) He questioned the fact that Mandy, in a very short work, gave Grandma three lines in a row in the final stanza (lines 10–12). The effect of this choice, to Jim, was to throw the poem out of balance (Was it possible that "I" said "Kids are having sex before their time"? But, no, that didn't make sense). And so on.

When (as we explain in more detail later on) "Grandma and Me" was circulated nationally to students in grades 7 to 12 and to preservice English language arts teachers, it was universally well received. Given nine or ten poems to rate, to either include in or drop from what was (at the time) a hypothetical anthology for young readers, both adolescents and preservice teachers chose this poem over some worthy challengers. We concluded that Jim's misgivings were irrelevant. Here was a poem with strong voice, with kid appeal, with bite. So we selected it over others that some might believe were better poems.

Developmental Tasks as a Basis for Curriculum Design

We credit Barbara Stanford and, indirectly, Robert Havighurst for shaping our thinking about how to structure *Poems by Adolescents and Adults*. In a *Media and Methods* article, Stanford (1971) made a case for organizing secondary curriculum around the built-in developmental needs of adolescents. She showed how these needs might be shaped into thematic elective courses or teaching units with a high degree of kid appeal.

Developmental tasks had been defined and elaborated by Havighurst in *Developmental Tasks and Education* (1948/1972). The needs that Havighurst termed *developmental tasks* included "achieving economic independence," "developing and refining a value system," and "achieving emotional independence from parents and other adults." More specifically, a developmental task is one that is insistent at a given stage of chronological and cognitive development. Thus an infant instinctively perceives the need to learn how to stand and walk, a preschooler instinctively perceives the need to dress and feed himself or herself, and an adolescent instinctively perceives the need to understand how his or her body is developing and maturing.

Along with the instinctive need to accomplish a developmental task comes a powerful interest in doing so. Infants want to grow into toddlerdom, toddlers want to become successful preschoolers, and early adolescents want to accomplish those things that older youth and younger adults can do.

Thus Barbara Stanford, in her proposal of a series of student-centered thematic courses intended to mesh well with developmental tasks, exploited what one might call *a developmental imperative*. Among her themes were "The Sociology of the High School," "The Responsible Use of Drugs," "Training and Care of the Body," "Masks and the Search for Human Identity," and "Male and Female."

Though transformed in a number of respects, Stanford's courses were the original basis for themes we used in building *Poems by Adolescents and Adults*. This is to say that we had in mind a set of themes and looked for poems that addressed them. Once we began reviewing submissions, though, we found it necessary to shape and/or re-form them. We learned, for example, that adolescents are no more likely than adults to write to a theme. Among the early discards were submissions from young people whose teachers, it seemed, said something to the effect of "They're looking for poems on gender or family relationships, so please write poems about those themes." (These poems—one might call them *compliance verse*—weren't very good, to say the least.) We also determined that one of Stanford's suggested themes, "The Responsible Use of Drugs," may have been a hot topic in the 1970s but was probably out of step with the relatively conservative views of the current day.

Determining to Create a Unique Poetry Anthology

In 1996–97, we worked with Hal Foster of the University of Akron on "Poetry Mission Possible," a national survey of teachers regarding how they planned poetry lessons. The three of us presented our findings at the 1997 NCTE Spring Conference in Charlotte. In the midst of this work, we discussed what we regarded then (and now) as a scarcity of student-centered poetry collections for young readers. We agreed, as well, that teachers should use poems written by adolescents much more than they do, because, other things being equal, what young people write is innately appealing to middle and high schoolers. On a related topic, we discussed the notion that the typical distinction English teachers make between student writing and the fiction and poems of established authors may be a false one. Why, we wondered, don't teachers place the poems of Robert Frost and Gwendolyn Brooks alongside those of poems from the school literary magazine or, for that matter, those written in class? Why do so many teachers act as if literature is something "out there," written by "writers" rather than by real people? Why don't teachers see that poems and stories produced in class are also "literature"?

Out of this conversation we—Dawnelle and Jim—decided to develop a unique collection of poems, a collection organized around student-centered themes, a collection that would freely mix poems by young people with those of adults at about a two-to-one ratio. That summer, we submitted a grant proposal to ALAN to support our work.

Between October 1997 and the NCTE Annual Convention in Detroit, we developed a plan for promoting *Poems by Adolescents and Adults* among middle-level and secondary English teachers. We prepared fliers for distribution at NCTE conferences—one thousand at the Detroit convention and a like number at the 1998 Albuquerque spring conference—and we prepared a mailing to selected NCTE leaders.

In Detroit, encouraged by chair Alan Olds, we met with the Advisory Committee of NCTE's Program to Recognize Excellence in Student Literary Magazines. Committee members suggested ways to approach (and *not* to approach) English teachers about gathering student submissions. They recognized ALAN's support as a plus, if, along with making this connection clear, we emphasized that students would not have to pay for a poem to be selected, in which case teachers would be more favorably disposed to ask students to participate. Among other topics addressed during this meeting was how best to acquire permission-to-publish statements and how we should set the age range for students submitting their work.[3] As a group, the committee voiced considerable support for the endeavor.

In December, we sent a call for submissions to approximately two hundred NCTE members: selected affiliate officers, editors of state and regional affiliate publications, members of the NCTE network who, annually in each state or Canadian province, recruit judges for NCTE's Program to Recognize Excellence in Student Literary Magazines. The mailing included a cover letter and one-page flier. On the flier's reverse side was an entry form with space for permission-to-publish statements from both the student and a parent. The flier advised entrants to provide postage if they wanted notification of a rejection.

The most helpful publicity for the anthology project came through a January 1998 *English Journal* call for submissions and a similar announcement in the winter/spring issue of the *ALAN Review*. Additional publicity came through e-mail announcements to NCTE-talk (an NCTE listserv) and through the distribution of fliers at various affiliate conferences from January through May of 1998.

Processing and Evaluating Submissions

We received submissions to *Poems by Adolescents and Adults* at Columbus State University. Upon receiving each poem, we assigned it a control number and letter (A, B, or C, depending on whether the student submitted one, two, or three poems). Thus, for example, the number and code letter 121B would be assigned to the second poem submitted by the 121st student poet.

By the June 1 postmark deadline, 835 students had submitted 1,637 poems. They represented thirty-eight states, four Canadian provinces, and Okinawa. Teachers played a major role in gathering and organizing submissions. A majority of submissions arrived in large envelopes with school return addresses; in each envelope were poems from as many as twenty or thirty students.

In order to rate the poems, we used straightforward criteria. We wanted short poems with strong and/or original voice, with memorable or fresh language, with skillful use of poetic conventions, and with connections to a theme we planned to use as a cluster in the collection. Our overarching criterion was that poems we picked should have what we called, for lack of a better term, "kid appeal"—that is, we wanted poems that were readily accessible to most adolescents, that captured a youthful experience or perspective, and that were short rather than long.

We evaluated submissions quickly and independently of one another. We rated poems as "N" (meaning *no* or *no way*), "Po" (meaning *possible for inclusion*), or "Pr" (meaning *probable for inclusion*). Then we compared ratings, discussed our frequent differences, and shifted poems from "Po" to "N" or "Pr" ratings. Our ratings became increasingly similar as we worked through the summer months. As June turned to July and then August, we each became more aware of (and respectful toward) how the other would apply our criteria.

We were assisted in the rating process by Claudia Wells and Tom Perry, veteran secondary English teachers from Columbus, Georgia, with twenty-eight and eight years experience, respectively, who added their ratings to ours. This process provided a third and sometimes a fourth perspective using the "N," "Po," and "Pr" system. Tom helped by skimming approximately two hundred poems we'd tentatively identified as *possibles* and suggested those he would be most likely to reassess as *probables* or, on the other hand, drop from consideration.

Ratings by Panels of Seventh- through Twelfth-Grade Students and Preservice Teachers

Between June and August of 1998, we recruited classroom teachers and English teacher preparation faculty to help further narrow the pool of *possible* and *probable* poems to about one hundred, the number we believed most suitable for *Poems by Adolescents and Adults*. By late August, seven English teachers (from North Carolina, Michigan, California, Georgia, and Minnesota) agreed that, when the school year began, they would ask their students to participate in a forced-choice rating of poems we had judged as *possibles*. Similarly, seven teacher educators (from Alabama, Texas, Florida, and Georgia) agreed to ask their students, preservice English language arts teachers, to participate in the same exercise.

The forced-choice exercise was reasonably simple. Students and preservice teachers selected, from a packet of nine to eleven poems, the three that they would be most likely to keep in an anthology and the three that they would be most likely to drop. In all instances, participants in the exercise, working in pairs or collaborative small groups, were encouraged to make their decisions by consensus rather than by simply voting. Report forms provided space for comments on each poem, whether it was rated *keep, drop,* or *no decision.*

A late-August mailing to these volunteers included a cover letter, a set of instructions, a criteria sheet, a packet of student poems, a report form, and a return envelope. Information about each young poet—that is, name, gender, grade level, school, and home town—was removed from poems in the packet.

From the report forms, returned by early October, we laid out student and preservice teacher ratings in these three categories:

+ (*keep*)

0 (*no decision*)

- (*drop*)

We used these ratings to help shape but not to dictate our final choices of student poems. To be sure, high ratings from both students and preservice teachers tipped the scales in favor of some poems that, without the ratings, we would have discarded. Similarly, negative ratings from both groups were hard to ignore.

From the outset, however, we knew we would make our own decisions regarding which poems to include. We emphasized to all that the project was not a contest or competition; rather, it was a way to gather good poems which, collectively, would make an excellent theme-based anthology.

We met in October and November of 1998 to make final selections. Following the winter holidays, we wrote letters to ninety-seven young poets ranging from a lone fifth grader to forty-one high school seniors conveying good news: their poems were among those selected for publication in *Poems by Adolescents and Adults*. Two young people—Gina Marie Damiano, an eleventh grader from Monmouth Junction, New Jersey, and Lindsey Blackburn, a senior from Norman, Oklahoma—had three poems selected. Four adolescents—David Clark (grade 12, Papillion, Nebraska), David Darst (grade 10, Greenwich, Connecticut), Derik Gummesen (grade 12, Salmon Arm, British Columbia), and Tara Ritchie (grade 7, Grand Junction, Colorado)—had two poems selected. The remaining young poets had one poem each. After receiving our acceptance letter, one decided that, for reasons of privacy, she did not want her poem published; we subsequently pulled it.

Selecting Adult Poems

We began selecting contemporary adult poems for *Poems by Adolescents and Adults* early in 1998. We wanted to use underanthologized poems rather than those frequently published in textbooks—for example, in reviewing poems by William Stafford, we avoided his well-known "Traveling Through the Dark" and "Freedom" in favor of the less well known "A Farewell, Age 10." Needing several adult poems to place in each theme, we looked for high-quality shorter poems that would be accessible to young readers, both in terms of their stylistic complexity and in what they said.

For several months, we gathered, shared, and subsequently evaluated published poems from an array of sources: discount and used bookstores, libraries, obscure literary journals, small poetry magazines—even yard sales. Our friends recommended still others. We turned to well-known poets such as William Stafford, Nikki Giovanni, and Gary Soto. Along the way we discovered other engaging word wizards such as Birmingham poet Charles Ghigna and Kathi Appelt, whose *Just People* (1997) was a 1998 ALA Best Book for Young Adults. Jim became interested in Appelt when he heard her presentation at the 1997 NCTE Annual Convention.

We tried to avoid collections of poems originally published for younger readers. An exception was Ruth Gordon's anthology *Pierced by a Ray of Sun: Poems about the Times We Feel Alone* (1995). We selected two poems—"Beating Up Billie Murphy in Fifth Grade" by Kathleen Aguero and "Recipe" by Janice Mirikitani—found in Gordon's anthology. We also picked three poems found in *American Sports Poems*, edited by R. R. Knudsen and May Swenson (1988).

Before long, we realized that we were replete with adult poems in some areas (love and family relations, for example) but needed more in others (such as school life and gender). Serendipitously, it would seem, we turned to *English Journal*, a rich source that, in the vernacular, was right under our noses. Reviewing all poems published by *English Journal* in the 1990s, we identified a substantial number that not only filled in some of our gaps but also were, on balance, superior to some poems we had already tentatively chosen. The final set of forty-three adult poems includes twenty-three that appeared first in *English Journal*.

Characteristics of Student Submissions

As we separated *probable* and *possible* poems from the larger mass of less effective work, we made a number of informal observations about the characteristics of the 1,637 poems that we received by the June 1, 1998, deadline. Here, in capsule form, is what we noticed:

◆ Poems from the fifty to one hundred adolescents who seemed to regard themselves as writers or poets were among the earliest and latest submissions. We were more likely to pick their work for eventual publication. These adolescents submitted their own poems—one, two, or three of them—using forms provided by their English teacher. Many attached self-addressed stamped envelopes to learn as soon as possible of our decision.

◆ We were most likely to rate poems from elective writing or creative writing classes as *probable* and *possible;* similarly, these poems were most likely to earn *keep* ratings by student and preservice teacher panels. They showed greater evidence of thorough and thoughtful writing.

◆ Poems that, we hypothesized, were the products of a class assignment in regular English classes were weaker overall than those submitted by individual adolescents or by young people in creative writing classes. These poems, which made up the majority of submissions, included occasional pearls that we selected for publication, but, more often than not, poems coming from six, sixteen, or twenty-six students in a single English class seemed to be the product of compliance rather than of commitment to the task of creating a poem or communicating an idea.

◆ Judging by their work alone, many if not most of the 835 adolescents submitting poems to *Poems by Adolescents and Adults* regard poetry (and life) as serious business, as rhymed no matter what, and as replete with abstract words rather than sensory language. Too few poems, in our view, had any sort of "twist" or surprise. Too many had a somber, even glum, voice. For many adolescents, word processing opened up the possibility of centering their work on the page, a very popular formatting ploy.

◆ Approximately 70 percent of submissions came from girls; 30 percent came from boys.

Characteristics of Poems Chosen for Publication

Poems by Adolescents and Adults includes 107 student poems. These are general characteristics of the collection:

◆ Twenty poems (19 percent) rhyme; the remaining eighty-seven poems (81 percent) do not. This reflects our taste as well as the taste of the two veteran English teachers who assisted us with the initial screening, the preferences of the seventh- to twelfth-grade students who participated in the forced-choice rating of *possible* poems, and the assessment in the same forced-choice rating by preservice English teachers.

◆ Twenty-six poems we selected are by boys (24 percent); the remaining eighty-one poems (76 percent) are by girls. This disparity exists despite our effort to balance the collection between males and females.

◆ The poems we selected for publication represent twenty-six states plus British Columbia:

16 poems	Michigan
10 poems	Georgia, New Jersey
7 poems	British Columbia
6 poems	Pennsylvania
5 poems	Colorado, Oklahoma, Texas
4 poems	Connecticut, Illinois, Maryland, Nebraska
3 poems	Louisiana, Missouri, Washington
2 poems	California, Idaho, Kentucky, New Hampshire, New York, North Carolina
1 poem	Massachusetts, New Mexico, Ohio, Utah, Virginia, Wyoming

High numbers from Michigan are linked, we believe, to the fact that the 1997 NCTE Annual Convention took place in Detroit and that many fliers promoting the anthology were distributed there. Similarly, we publicized the project extensively in Georgia, Jim's home state, including at a February 1998 Georgia Council of Teachers of English conference attended by one thousand teachers.

- Because students did not indicate their ethnicity on submission forms, we had no way to determine that characteristic of the writers of the 107 student poems selected for publication.

- The poems we selected for publication represent a substantial age and grade range, as follows:

Grade 5	1 poem
Grade 6	7 poems
Grade 7	9 poems
Grade 8	9 poems
Grade 9	12 poems
Grade 10	15 poems
Grade 11	15 poems
Grade 12	39 poems

Obviously, there is a gradual increase in the frequency of poems, by grade, as one moves from grade 5 to grade 6, grade 7, and so on. We chose nearly as many poems by seniors as by students in grades 9 through 11 combined. We find ourselves speculating about why this should be the case. One possible reason is the greater likelihood that seniors enroll in elective creative writing classes, submit their writing to school literary magazines, and so forth. Beyond this, it may be that seniors who hope to attend selective-admissions colleges and universities are more inclined to participate in writing contests and similar events than are younger students. Finally, although we did not tally submissions by grade, it may also be that more seniors (for either or both of the two reasons cited above) submitted their poems to *Poems by Adolescents and Adults* than did younger students.

We believe that the poems written by students in the middle school or junior high set are as "good" as those written by juniors and seniors. At no point did we select a poem while reasoning, "Let's use this one. It's really good *for an eighth grader*." Rather, our reasoning was more likely to be this: "Let's use this one. It's really good, *and* it's by an eighth grader who uses language marvelously well." Similarly, for those poems rated by seventh- to twelfth-grade students and preservice English language arts teachers, we did not identify them by grade level, gender, or geographic location. As a result, positive ratings were based on perceptions of the poems themselves and not on characteristics of the young poets.

How to Use These Poems: Classroom Teachers

Ours is not a book of activities, lessons, or teaching units. Simply put, we've provided the poems, and we'll rely on resourceful teachers to design the activities, to implement the lessons, and to create the instructional units that will make good use of poems from this collection. In Appendixes A, B, and C, we highlight excellent book, periodical, and online resources that teachers can turn to for teaching strategies. We especially recommend recent NCTE publications such as Judith Rowe Michaels's *Risking Intensity: Reading and Writing Poetry with High School Students* (1999) and Albert B. Somers's *Teaching Poetry in High School* (1999) as excellent sources for teaching strategies to use with poetry.

Here, though, we make several broad suggestions. Based on these ideas, classroom teachers may decide to use poems from *Poems by Adolescents and Adults* in one or more of these ways:

Use poems in the collection with thematic units or as companion pieces to selected works of literature. In our section introductions, we link each theme to the classics as well as to contemporary adolescent literature. Poems from the "School Life" section might be linked to works ranging from J. D. Salinger's *The Catcher in the Rye* to Katherine Paterson's *The Great Gilly Hopkins*. Is school truly a "children's jail," as student poet Derik Gummesen claims? Would Holden Caulfield agree? Is there more to "another average girl" (as depicted by Jennifer Patterson) than meets the eye?

Skillful teachers can use Poems by Adolescents and Adults *to integrate their teaching across genres and topics.*

Use poems in the collection as occasional pieces that mesh with current events or with events tied to the school calendar. Poems in the collection deal with everything from food in the school cafeteria to prom night, from homelessness to the environment, from war in faraway places to violence in schools far too close to home. The right poems at the right moment—read aloud, discussed, posted on a bulletin board—can open up student thinking and tie the literary arts to life. Teachers sometimes lose sight of these ties.

Skillful teachers can use Poems by Adolescents and Adults *to ensure that what kids learn in their classrooms is about life as much as it is about literature.*

Use poems in this collection as a springboard for student exploration of contemporary poets and their work. Many poems by William Stafford, Nikki Giovanni, Gary Soto, and others will appeal to today's adolescents. Stafford, with his dogged social consciousness, focuses on human relationships and on the linkage between people and the environment (see "A Farewell, Age Ten" in the "Gender" section). Giovanni explores human relations and social issues in an unmistakable voice marked by skillful use of African American vernacular (e.g., "A Poem for Flora," "Housecleaning," and "A Poem of Friendship"). Soto, who is well known for his young adult novels and who was a 1997 National Book Award finalist in poetry, creates verse for both young people and adults; his "Behind Grandma's House" (in the "Masks and the Search for Identity" section) is a vivid recollection of childhood, yet it speaks to larger issues of self-definition.

Skillful teachers can use Poems by Adolescents and Adults *to move kids beyond poems selected by textbook anthologists, however good those poems may be.*

Use poems in the collection as models for student writing. What better way to stimulate good writing by students than exposing them to other good writing by students? Many poems in this collection are rich in sensory detail (see, for example, Lucy Dupree's "Shoes" or Tiffany Trawick's "Drawn"), and, through close observation, others might use them as stepping-off points for their own work. Mandy Glover's "Grandma and Me" is an amusing dialogue between two willful voices. What sort of dialogues might students capture on paper between teacher and student, coach and athlete, or mother and father? In a similar vein, poems by well-known adult poets can also serve as models for student writing.

Inevitably, teachers will regard some of these poems as more wonderful than others. Those that are *less* wonderful, we suggest, can still serve to stimulate good—or better—student writing. Teachers need to pose these questions: Does this poem use fresh language? Offer a unique insight? Capture an experience powerfully? What about *this* poem? What does it do that the other doesn't?

Skillful teachers can use Poems by Adolescents and Adults *to help adolescents develop a repertoire of different poetic forms, voices, and techniques.*

Use poems in the collection to help students explore the nature of contemporary verse. Poetry, in the vernacular, "ain't what it used to be." Or is it? Helping young people experience the full range of contemporary poetry—helping them rise above stereotypical ideas regarding what poetry is, what it's about, and how it communicates—is a challenge that teachers should welcome.

In the past twenty to thirty years, American poetry has undergone a renaissance. It is far more accessible, far less the turf only of English majors and their professors, than was the case in the past. Poetry shows up in rap, in country music, in rock lyrics. In New York City, poetry has been placarded on buses and subways.[4] It's likely to be read aloud tonight by earnest teenagers and accountants at your local Barnes and Noble bookstore or your neighborhood coffee shop.

Devised in the mid-eighties by Chicago poet Marc Smith, the poetry slam has captured the imagination of young and not-so-young poetry enthusiasts from all parts of the country (see, for example, www.poetryslam.com). In a slam, poets, either individually or as an ensemble, perform their work before five randomly selected audience members. Though it won't ever be an Olympic sport, poetry slam has its own annual national competition, its own stars, its own culture.

In keeping with the range of contemporary American poetry, the poems collected here are about topics as diverse as exercise (Kristen Haver's "Twenty-Five Minutes on the Stairmaster"), teaching a child to ride a bicycle (Jerrol Leiter's "Learning to Ride"), and eating disorders (Allison Stevens's "I Used to Try Not to Look Down"). Yet they are also about traditional topics and themes such as love, friendship, and nature. Poems in this collection capture settings as diverse as school stairways (Kathi Appelt's "That Kiss"), Laundromats (Rachel Devenish's "Coin Laundry"), and a boy's first car (Jeremy Casey's "Love, Such a Wonderful Thing"). Others are set in presumably "poetic" places such as gardens, woods, and seashores. Some poems presented here rhyme; many do not. All—well, almost all—use compression, the poet's gift of capturing what is big and profound concisely and powerfully.

Skillful teachers can use Poems by Adolescents and Adults *to help adolescents broaden their ideas about poetry and about how, as an art form, it relates to their everyday lives.*

How to Use These Poems: Teacher Educators

We believe that teacher educators can also do good things with poems from this collection. Jim's teachers-in-training at Columbus State University are already building plans around student poems, linking them to works of adolescent literature, and sharing them with seventh- to twelfth-grade students during student teaching.

Among the more obvious possibilities for teacher educators who want to use *Poems by Adolescents and Adults* are these:

- ◆ As they plan lessons and instructional units, encourage teacher candidates to incorporate poems from this collection. How, for example, might a teacher use Shannon Iezzi's "It's Only a Tattoo" to stimulate thinking and talk about parent/child conflicts and roles? What works of literature, contemporary or traditional, reflect similar conflicts, or their absence?

- ◆ Use poems from the collection as the basis for microteaching or simulated lessons. Ask candidates to speculate on what approach they might take in discussing Crystal Gossard's "Prom Night" or Janice Mirikitani's "Recipe" with their students. What should be brought out—aspects of technique and style, life connections, or what? Should the lesson flow in directions that students initiate, or should teachers prompt certain kinds of thinking and response?

- ◆ Ask these questions of teacher candidates: What typical (or atypical) concerns of today's teenagers are captured by these poems?

What controversial topics do they address? How do poems by middle schoolers compare with those by high school students, by adolescents almost ready for college? How, for example, does the language of younger poets compare with that of more mature teenagers?

What We've Learned

We've learned a great deal. We've learned that, at a point in our culture when English teachers are neck-deep in print and electronic information, it is difficult but certainly possible—even in six months—to publicize a worthy project on a national basis. We've affirmed our knowledge that committed English teachers—from Harris County Middle School, just north of where Jim works at Columbus State University, from the North Carolina School of Science and Mathematics near Dawnelle's home in Durham, from as far away as Salmon Arm, British Columbia, three thousand miles to the northwest—teachers from these communities and scores of others can be counted on to take the extra step to help talented young people have a chance to see their work in print. Most of all, we've affirmed our belief that young people, through using language well, can touch us, amuse us, surprise us with both their human savvy and their ways with words.

Conclusion

We began our anthology project with three beliefs: that poetry by adolescents is an untapped resource for classroom use, that teachers should frequently use poems by adolescents and adults alongside one another, and that—if we gathered good poems from young people and clustered them thematically alongside good poems by adult poets—we could create a unique resource for middle school and secondary English teachers. We conclude with satisfaction in our product, as well as considerable delight in the fact that it is now on its way to teachers and kids, where it will do the most good.

Notes

1. We owe several of our theme titles to Barbara Stanford (1971), who proposed a curriculum organized around developmental tasks. Two of our themes ("Masks and the Search for Identity" and "Individual, Group, Crowd") come directly from Stanford's proposal. Others ("Gender," "Generations," and "Choices, Choices, Choices," for example) emerged as we reviewed poems.

2. As you examine *Poems by Adolescents and Adults* further, you'll learn more about us. In each theme-based cluster of poems in the collection, we've included short personal reflections based on our own experiences as teenagers or as teachers working with teenagers. Poetry, we know, is a highly personal mode of discourse. Our own reflections, we believe, serve to further humanize the poetry we have selected in each section.

3. Although *Poems by Adolescents and Adults* emphasizes *adolescent* appeal, we agreed that submissions might come from any public or private school student who had not, as of the end of the 1997–98 school year, graduated or finished grade 12. In fact, we received submissions from children as young as age nine (fourth grade).

4. See *Poetry in Motion: 100 Poems from the Subways and Buses*, edited by Molly Peacock, Elise Paschen, and Neil Neches (New York: Norton, 1996).

References

Appelt, K. (1997). *Just people and other poems for young readers & Paper/pen/poem: A young writer's way to begin.* Houston: Absey.

Draper. S. M. (1997). *Buttered bones: Collected poetry.* Cincinnati: Author.

Dunning, S., Lueders, E., Nye, N. S., Gilyard, K., & Worley, D. A. (Eds.). (1995). *Reflections on a gift of watermelon pickle and other modern verse.*

Dunning, S., Lueders, E., & Smith, H. (Eds.). (1966). *Reflections on a gift of watermelon pickle and other modern verse.* Glenview, IL: Scott, Foresman.

Giovanni, N. (1974). *My house: Poems.* New York: Morrow.

Giovanni, N. (1978). *Cotton candy on a rainy day: Poems*. New York: Morrow.

Gordon, R.(Ed.). (1995). *Pierced by a ray of sun: Poems about the times we feel alone*. New York: HarperCollins.

Havighurst, R. J. (1972). *Developmental tasks and education* (3rd ed.). New York: Longman. (First edition published 1948)

Janeczko, P. B. (1993). *Looking for your name: A collection of contemporary poems*. New York: Orchard Books.

Janeczko. P. B. (1995). *Wherever home begins: 100 contemporary poems*. New York: Orchard Books.

Knudson, R. R., and Swenson, M. (Eds.). (1988). *American sports poems*. New York: Orchard Books.

Michaels, J. R. (1999). *Risking intensity: Reading and writing poetry with high school students*. Urbana, IL: NCTE.

Myers, W. D. (1993). *Brown angels: An album of pictures and verse*. New York: HarperCollins.

Peck, R. (Ed.). (1970) *Sounds and silences: Poetry for now*. New York: Dell.

Peck, R. (Ed.). (1971). *Mindscapes: Poems for the real world*. New York: Dell.

Peck, R. (Ed.). (1976). *Pictures that storm inside my head: Poems for the inner you*. New York: Avon.

Somers, A. B. (1999). *Teaching poetry in high school*. Urbana, IL: NCTE.

Soto, G. (1990). *A fire in my hands: A book of poems*. New York: Scholastic.

Soto, G. (1992). *Neighborhood odes*. San Diego: Harcourt Brace Jovanovich.

Stanford, B. (1971). How innovators fail. *Media and Methods, 8*(2), 26–35.

PART I

AT HOME: THE PERSON, THE FAMILY

CHAPTER ONE

Masks and the Search for Identity

Observant teachers are aware that "Who am I?" is the most important—and most difficult—question facing most adolescents. Giving this question careful thought is natural to adolescents. Not doing so is easier, perhaps, but taking the more reflective, difficult path leads to growth and maturity.

In childhood, one's identity is determined more often than not by country, neighborhood, and family—as well as by sex, racial background, religion, and geographic region. At the age of eight or ten, few children step back from their lives and wonder about their identity. In adolescence, though, one sees young people raising questions about their personal identity. They may turn away from their parents' values, they may rebel against rules at home and at school that seem arbitrary, or they may reject roles that others have determined for them without first asking, "What do you think? What are you like, really? What do you want to be, both now and tomorrow?"

Many young people supplant the norms of their family and community with those of their friends, wearing the same clothes, talking the same talk, possibly even thinking the same thoughts. Adults become rankled by kids who wear what grown-ups regard as outlandish clothes, pierce their bodies, and dye their hair every color of the rainbow.

We believe that the English classroom is an ideal place for young people to address the "Who am I?" question, to reflect on their values, and to read high-quality literature through which, vicariously at least, they may test out unfamiliar roles, identities, and lifestyles. Skillful English teachers should help teenagers reflect on these and related issues in order to form more mature, thoughtful conceptions of personal identity. As often as not, the result of such classroom inquiry is an affirmation of familial and cultural norms coupled with a better understanding of both themselves and other young people.

Literature is peppered with young characters seeking answers to the "Who am I?" question. Traditional American and British literature brings to mind Huck Finn as he wrestles with his conscience when he and Jim encounter bounty-hunting slave catchers, or *The Catcher in the Rye*'s Holden Caulfield as he is tossed out of yet another school, or, on her balcony, Shakespeare's Juliet—lamenting that Romeo's family identity makes them enemies by birth—asking, "What's in a name?"

Characters in young adult literature are often engaged in an intense search for their identity. If teachers want to nudge their students toward such self-exploration, they might introduce younger readers to Margaret in Judy Blume's *Are You There God? It's Me, Margaret*. For high school students—boys in particular—teachers might introduce them to Chris Lynch's three-volume Blue-Eyed Son series and to Mick, its title character. Mick finds that extricating himself from the boozy violence of his Boston family is easier said than done. Still other adolescent readers will want to explore what Em Thurkill accomplishes against great odds in Norma Fox Mazer's *When She Was Good*, or how Slam (in Walter Dean Myers's novel of the same name) tries to balance school, basketball, and a talent for photography. These novels would form a solid core of readings in a unit exploring identity.

In a culture as diverse as that of the contemporary United States, one's ethnic heritage gives a young person a base on which to build a personal identity even as it may create dissonance between one's roots and her or his present and future. Our students—whether they come from a nominal minority or from a "mainstream" group—have made powerful connections with two novels: Chaim Potok's *The Chosen*, relating the experiences of a Jewish boy in Brooklyn in the 1940s, and Sandra Cisneros's *The House on Mango Street*, telling of life for a Latino family in Chicago during the 1950s and 1960s. We are also impressed by two recent short story collections—*An Island Like You*, by Judith Cofer, and *American Eyes*, edited by Lori Carlson—as they examine cultural transitions for Puerto Rican Americans and Asian Americans. Lensey Namioka's *April and the Dragon Lady* addresses similar issues for Chinese Americans.

Poets who contributed to this section, "Masks and the Search for Identity," have asked—and sometimes answered—the "Who am I?" question. Gary Soto ("Behind Grandma's House") recalls how much of his identity derives from his Mexican American heritage. Gina Marie Damiano reveals how adolescents, girls in particular, may be "a creamy mixture of you, of me, of her" ("Pretty Parcel"), and, in "Poem for Flora," Nikki Giovanni contrasts the experience of being considered "colored and ugly" with that of the Bible's Sheba, who was "black and comely." In "You're Who?" Heather Miser recognizes what a powerful influence popular culture exerts on the way young people act and think.

Reminiscences

Jim: I remember starting tenth grade. My family had moved from one side of the county to the other. I was changing schools and wanted to fit in with the other guys. I was a fat kid, not an athlete. On the first day, I wore clothes that I figured would make a statement about who I was, how with-it I was, how fashionable. Early in the summer, I'd bought these jazzy pants in downtown Washington at a store where they sold zoot suits. They were gray khakis, and they had this two-inch stripe down each leg that looked like black-and-white leopard skin, spots and all.

Well, I wore those jazzy, leopardy pants that one day—and maybe one other time—but I could tell that at my new school the statement I was making was all wrong. Trying to be hip, I'd turned out to be square, square, square.

Dawnelle: From second grade on, I remember viewing myself as somehow "different" from the other kids. Everyone else, it seemed, was into sports, socializing, shopping, boyfriends, hanging out at the movies—anything outside of school. While I enjoyed many of those things, too, I was drawn to school and school-like endeavors. I read prolifically, tried my hand at writing (with much encouragement from my teachers), and hung out with the Hickory Choral Society, a classical choral group that I fell in love with when I attended one of their concerts as a seventh grader.

By middle school, I tried to hide all of my real interests, opting instead to try to fit into the mainstream. My ultimate goal was to become "popular," to integrate myself into the in-group so that I wouldn't be "found out." I wore all of the "right" clothes, got a haircut, pretended to be more interested than I was in popular music groups of the time, and even kept a relationship with Jeff, my first love, longer than I wanted to just so I could say I had a boyfriend. Of course, the "real Dawnelle" shone through all along. Once I realized this—once I knew that who I was would come to the surface no matter what—toward the end of my high school years, I felt truly liberated. Interestingly enough, when I took off my mask, I started noticing others accepting me for who I was.

Poet's Explanation

See Nikki Giovanni's explanation on why and how she wrote "Poem for Flora" on page 40.

References

Blume, J. (1991). *Are you there God? It's me, Margaret.* New York: Dell. (Original work published 1970)

Carlson, L. M. (1994). *American eyes: New Asian-American short stories for young adults.* New York: Fawcett Juniper.

Cisneros, S. (1984). *The house on Mango Street.* Houston: Arte Publico. (Original work published 1983)

Cofer, J. O. (1995). *An island like you: Stories of the barrio.* New York: Orchard Books.

Lynch, C. (1996a). *Blood relations* (Blue-eyed son series 2). New York: HarperCollins.

Lynch, C. (1996b). *Dog eat dog* (Blue-eyed son series 3). New York: HarperTrophy.

Lynch, C. (1996c). *Mick* (Blue-eyed son series 1). New York: HarperCollins.

Mazer, N. F. (1997). *When she was good*. New York: Scholastic.

Myers, W. D. (1996). *Slam!* New York: Scholastic.

Namioka, L. (1994). *April and the Dragon Lady*. San Diego: Browndeer Press.

Potok, C. (1995). *The chosen*. New York: Fawcett. (Original work published 1967)

Salinger, J. D. (1991). *The catcher in the rye*. New York: Little, Brown. (Original work published 1951)

Behind Grandma's House

At ten I wanted fame. I had a comb
And two Coke bottles, a tube of Bryl-cream.
I borrowed a dog, one with
Mismatched eyes and a happy tongue,
And wanted to prove I was tough
In the alley, kicking over trash cans,
A dull chime of tuna cans falling.
I hurled light bulbs like grenades
And men teachers held their heads,
Fingers of blood lengthening
On the ground. I flicked rocks at cats,
Their goofy faces spurred with foxtails.
I kicked fences. I shooed pigeons.
I broke a branch from a flowering peach
And frightened ants with a stream of spit.
I said "*Chale*," "In your face," and "No way

Daddy-O" to an imaginary priest
Until grandma came into the alley,
Her apron flapping in a breeze,
Her hair mussed, and said, "Let me help you,"
And punched me between the eyes.

Gary Soto
New and Selected Poems

On Gary Soto

We are true Gary Soto fans—whether it's his poetry, his fiction, or his autobiographical nonfiction. Among our favorites are *Jesse* (Harcourt Brace, 1994), *Neighborhood Odes* (Harcourt Brace Jovanovich, 1992), *Living Up the Street: Narrative Recollections* (Dell, 1992), and *A Summer Life* (Dell, 1991). See also *A Natural Man* (1999, Chronicle Books) and *Junior College* (1997, Chronicle Books).

A Piece of Furniture

Move me. Dust me if
You care to.
Hide me in a corner.
Show me off for all to
See. I am the comfort zone.
Appreciated for
What I am worth. Invisible
For what I am useless.
Kick me. Polish
Me when company
Comes. Scratch me,
But ignore the eternal
Scar. I am all arms
And legs. Feel nothing. See
Nothing. Do nothing.
I absorb dirt. But I

Am sturdy. Sit on
Me if you will. I am
Quite sure I can survive
Beneath you.

Laura Beth Malick, 12th grade
North Penn High School
Lansdale, Pennsylvania

Pretty Parcel

Look at her.
See her skin, taut and thick,
neatly packaging her bones into
one simple scheme.

Just like her mind.

Look at her.
Her lips, immaculately glossed,
looking natural, yet prepared.

Just like her words.

"They surely broke the mold when they made her."
Lumps of vanity poured into
a creamy mixture
of you, of me, of her.
Two parts fabricated, one part futile.
Add some insult to injury,
beauty to taste.
Makes one girl, perfect for any occasion.
Self-assimilates for all your needs, never needing more than
some acceptance and a fashionable wardrobe.

Gina Marie Damiano, 11th grade
South Brunswick High School, Monmouth Junction, New Jersey

You're Who?

I am a Garbage Pail Kid
born in a gravel sandbox,
raised on the rusted swing set,
and deformed with scrapes, cuts and bruises covering elbows
    and knees.

I am a New Kid on the Block
Hangin' Tough, Step by Step
Hammer pants parachute around my legs each
jump from the
top rung of the monkey bars

I am the Pepsi Generation
my hair no longer crimped
my hat now turned straight instead of tilted to the right
and the blue eye shadow no longer smears my lids.

I am not a Miss America
It comes all natural here
No silicon boobs, liposuction, or tummy tucks.
My teeth are not vaselined and crystalline white.
My hair is straight and shiny
each strand having a life of its own
different from the glued and spritzed style on TV.

I am a Garbage Pail Kid, part of the Pepsi Generation, and will
    never be Miss America
but I may sometime become an intricate part of this century.
Platform shoes are back and so are big collars and bell
    bottoms.
The times might catch up with me yet.

Heather Miser, 12th grade
Papillion-LaVista High School, Papillion, Nebraska

I Used to Try Not to Look Down

I used to try not to look down,
Down at my legs
The way the fat on my thighs
Seemed miles away from bone
I tried not to feel fat,
After I ate
But with my stomach expanding,
One couldn't help but think
Did it stick out too much?
I used to wish I could leave my body
And float around for a while
Till that feeling passes
I would look down upon it
And not care what I saw
Because I wouldn't be part of it
And it wouldn't be part of me
I could have been free from this burden
But I couldn't do such a thing and I would sit there
And try not to see
The things I am imagining
Now I know
I am more
Than the size of my jeans.

Allison Stevens, 9th grade
Sherwood High School, Sandy Spring, Maryland

Play Pretend

We generalize
We dramatize
We exercise
We moralize

We speculate
We estimate
We conjugate
We congregate

We do it all
To pay the toll
To hurt us all
To kill the soul

So say
goodbye
To your soul and spirit
So let it fly
Pretend not to hear it

Jeremy Stoll, 10th grade
St. Mary Catholic Central
Monroe, Michigan

The Adolescent Essence

Three slim vials
Arranged neatly on the shelf.
Empathy, Sympathy, Apathy.

Three slim vials
Waiting softly to be felt.
Inaccuracy, Inferiority, Indifference.

Three slim vials
Easily spilled and overflowing,
Overused in the process of growing.

Gina Marie Damiano, 11th grade
South Brunswick High School
Monmouth Junction, New Jersey

Shadowed Thoughts

Remember the student
who tried suicide last spring?
You know, who
overdosed on pills
In the girls' bathroom,
She and her mom were
mad and not talking?

She had a baby today—
a boy.

Faye D. Christensen
English Journal (January 1991)

Unfortunately

all the things that I'm not
fall, like wet, dying
angels, cold outside
my window.
their eyes are shut—
and blind to rainbows
(I can no longer see
the people I could have—
should—
have been) their
halos drag rusted crowns
of disappointment, they are
dead thought.
for a second, one
resembles my mother
(hating the tattoo on my foot)
with raspberry hair
and gold-pecan fingertips
(my grades stole their flavor
also) and her eyes
are pleading prayers
when I could not catch
her, out
in the rain.

Amanda Gagliardi, 12th grade
Parkway North High School
St. Louis, Missouri

Chock-Full of You

The skin has stretched
over the swollen, bloated tumor
that is my belly.
Pallid putty encases
my plump insides
and the guts that spill down,
soggy with guilt,
are once again flooded with you.

A moment ago your voice was masked
by the crackle of the wrapper
as I struggled to free my aliment from
its plastic sheath.
Your lies dissolve with the morsels,
and slide down between chews.
The smooth 12 oz. boxes,
the glint of tattered wrappers,
and the sickly glow of the fluorescent light
hovering above my head like a halo
make up the perfect dynamics
to subdue you.

My fingers trace the fine hairs on my tummy
as I try to forget the relentless churning of my insides.
Mouthful after mouthful swelled my body
while my memory discarded your presence.
But the gut-wrenching aftermath has begun and once again,
I am chock-full
of you.

Gina Marie Damiano, 11th grade
South Brunswick High School, Monmouth Junction, New Jersey

An Answer to a Liberal's Question:
What Can I Do about Prejudice?

Darken your skin.
Go to a tanning salon or just stand in the wild heat.
Darken your skin, broaden your nose and fill out the
    dimensions of your lips.
Darken your skin, broaden your nose, and work on a
    plantation.
Darken your skin, work on a plantation and pick cotton and
    sugar cane until dusk.
Darken your skin, broaden your nose, fill out the dimensions
    of your lips, work on a plantation picking cotton and try
    to prosper.
Walk into a store.
Walk into a high-class store and look at everything in it.
Walk into a store with dark skin, broad nose, and full lips and
    let someone follow you.
Let the person ask you why you are in their store and tell them
    you are just looking.
Remember to darken your skin.
Become a parent.
Pass down your dark skin, broad nose and full lips.
Let people think that you are uneducated and living in poverty
    or on welfare.
Become a parent, be looked upon as poor and try to rise above
    the statistics.
Darken your skin, broaden your nose and lips.
Be looked upon as uneducated and poor and see if you under-
    stand.
No, you're not ready to face it.

Tykeria T. Muhammad, 9th grade
South Brunswick High School, Monmouth Junction, New Jersey

Poem for Flora

when she was little
and colored and ugly with short
straightened hair
and a very pretty smile
she went to Sunday school to hear
'bout nebuchadnezzar the king
of the jews

and she would listen

shadrach, meshach and abednego in the fire

and she would listen

how god was neither north
nor south cast or west
with no color but all
she remembered was that
Sheba was Black and comely

and she would think

i want to be
like that

Nikki Giovanni
The Men and the Women

Nikki Giovanni's Explanation of "Poem for Flora"

My mother has two best friends: Theresa and Flora. I almost don't remember when one or the other and mostly both was not at our dinner table or at least stopping by for a bit of lunch or breakfast on Saturday when Flora did her shopping or maybe for a glass of beer or two ("I believe I will," Flora would respond when Mommy offered). So I was always looking at these two women who epitomized what women and friendship would could mean. And I tried to put Flora who was a Baptist churchgoer into context whereas Theresa was a lapsed Catholic, so the cadence came up Southern rather than sonnet. And Sheba was a wonderful sharp very hip woman who was smart and desirable. And that was a good thing as far as I could tell.

CHAPTER TWO

Gender

The more time we teachers spend in schools, the more clearly we see that, for many adolescents, their sex—their identity as a male or female—is at the heart of their pursuit of the question "Who am I?" Anxieties about gender identity are both in-born—even instinctive—and reasoned. Regardless of their culture, younger human beings must find an agreeable place as adult men or women.

Defining and finding that "agreeable place" is a more complicated process today than it was thirty or forty years ago. Stereotyped ideas about what being female or male means are routinely challenged in the workplace, on the athletic field, and in the home. Simultaneously, greater openness about homosexuality—and a degree of tolerance for gays and lesbians—leads some adolescents to ponder the very basis of their sexuality.

Until the onset of puberty, kids typically look to their parents, teachers, sports heroes, singers, and other role models to discover what it means to be a "man" or a "woman." In our culture, young adolescent females discover cosmetics, fashion sense, and intellectual ability. Adolescent boys may turn to sports, music, and cars. Still others, male and female, resist or—some would say—rise above these stereotypes, muddying the waters of gender definition and claiming proudly, "Hey! I am a human being. Pure and simple."

Traditional and contemporary literature often presents young people, female and male, working toward feminine and masculine roles with which they can feel comfortable. In nineteenth-century literature (and, more recently, in the film version starring Winona Ryder and Susan Sarandon), Jo in Louisa May Alcott's *Little Women* is determined to be a writer, an occupation thought to be unsuited to middle-class young women in her times. In *Fair and Tender Ladies,* Southern novelist Lee Smith also traces a young girl's journey into adulthood, and through the various stages of life, in her depiction of Ivy Rowe, a remarkable Appalachian woman, from the age of fourteen into her nineties, and Alice Walker's *The Color Purple* recounts, among other things, Celie's journey toward understanding herself as a woman.

Teachers may also turn to many fine works of contemporary young adult literature in order to help students explore gender roles. Judy Blume's novels address various aspects of what it means to be female. Deenie, in the novel of the same name, taking self-awareness to the extreme, becomes so caught up in the idea that a true woman is petite and shapely that she risks her own health to become something that she is not. *Forever*, popular among adolescents of all ages, explores one girl's discovery of her sexual identity.

Sexual identity is also the focus of M. E. Kerr's widely read *Deliver Us from Evie*. Told from the perspective of Evie's younger brother, the novel is a skillful treatment of a farm family's gradual acceptance of Evie's homosexuality.

Karen Cushman's *Catherine, Called Birdy*, set in medieval England, causes young readers to think about how societal conceptions of the worth of females have changed between then and contemporary times. Birdy's efforts to avoid being married off by her father to a series of unlovable suitors are both entertaining and revealing. Deborah Savage's *To Race a Dream,* set in a very different time and place (contemporary Minnesota), presents another female going against the grain of family and community expectations: fifteen-year-old Theodora's parents cannot understand her ambition of becoming a harness-racing driver.

For boys, Walter Dean Myers's *Fast Sam, Cool Clyde, and Stuff* traces Stuff's journey through experiences that cause him to examine the question "What does it mean to be macho?" Belinda Hurmence's *A Girl Called Boy*, a time-travel novel, challenges traditional gender roles, making it clear that it is okay to be oneself even if this goes against the conventional gender grain.

Another recent novel that addresses this theme is Jerry Spinelli's *Wringer*. Ten-year-old Palmer doesn't see why it's his responsibility, as a boy, to wring the necks of wounded pigeons following the town's annual pigeon shoot. He displays great courage in standing up for what he believes is right and wrong.

David Klass's *California Blue* also examines male roles. The novel deals with the conflict between seventeen-year-old John, interested in biology and track, and his father, a logger and one-time football hero who has been diagnosed with cancer.

In the poems that follow, just as in Victorian and contemporary literature, we see a range of points of view about male and female roles. Charity Koon turns the gender tables upside down and, as a result, gets our attention with "Heart Attack." Both Roodabeh Samimi ("My Father Mows the Lawn") and Leah Lenk ("Electra") reflect on the conventional roles and responsibilities of men and women in our culture, as well as the rivalry that sometimes occurs between mothers and daughters. Joseph Ball's "Jenny Says" makes it clear that some among us don't appreciate "girls being girls" (whatever that may mean), and John Laue's "Around the High School" captures the rumbling masculinity of "boys being boys" in a familiar scene.

Reminiscences

Dawnelle: I grew up in a neighborhood where all the other kids were boys. We built outdoor forts, held fierce video game competitions, and tried our hand at football, soccer, and basketball. It was fun for a while, but by about fourth grade, and after several cases of shin splints, I was tired of this routine. I turned into something of a fashion queen instead, focusing most of my free time on new hair styles, pop rock musical crazes, and the latest clothing styles. I was delighted when, by seventh grade, my mom started letting me wear make-up—"just a little, honey"—and it became "cool" to wear dresses to school. I also turned to reading—everything from *Young Ms.* magazine to novels by Katherine Paterson, Beverly Cleary, and Judy Blume. As an adult recalling these times, I credit my mix of experiences—my dabbling in "boyhood" and "girlhood"—for my strong sense that it is powerful to acknowledge my womanhood, and that doing so need not prevent me from being and doing whatever means the most to me at any given time.

Jim: I didn't think much about being masculine (or not) when I was young. At a certain younger age, I played and hung out with both girls and boys. In Scouts, from about age eleven on, I spent more time with boys than girls and, now that I think about it, probably defined my view of masculinity from some of the leaders and other boys. My father, who seemed able to do just about anything he wanted to, became my hero at the time.

I also had a homosexual encounter in Scouts, which scared the heck out of me and affirmed my strong interest in the opposite sex. That, you might say, is another story entirely.

Because our high school was quite large, it was possible to avoid athletics and still be thought of as masculine. Boys, including stars of the football team, were involved in music and drama. That made me feel good for some reason.

Poets' Explanations

Conrad Hilberry comments on "Instruction" on page 50. Danielle Mangano explains "how the cookie crumbles (jane's sweet revenge)" on page 51.

References

Alcott, L. M. (1983). *Little women*. Los Angeles: Price Stern Sloan. (Original work published 1868, 1869)

Blume, J. (1973). *Deenie*. Scarsdale, NY: Bradbury.

Blume, J. (1975). *Forever*. Scarsdale, NY: Bradbury.

Cushman, K. (1994). *Catherine, called Birdy*. New York: Clarion Books.

Hurmence, B. (1990). *A girl called boy*. New York: Clarion Books. (Original work published 1982)

Kerr, M. E. (1995). *Deliver us from Evie*. New York: HarperTrophy. (Original work published 1994)

Klass, D. (1994). *California blue*. New York: Scholastic.

Myers, W. D. (1988). *Fast Sam, Cool Clyde, and Stuff*. New York: Viking. (Original work published 1975)

Savage, D. (1994). *To race a dream*. Boston: Houghton Mifflin.

Smith, L. (1989). *Fair and tender ladies*. New York: Ballantine Books. (Original work published 1988)

Spinelli, J. (1997). *Wringer*. New York: HarperCollins.

Walker, A. (1996). *The color purple*. New York: Pocket Books. (Original work published 1982)

A Farewell, Age Ten

While its owner looks away I touch the rabbit.
Its long soft ears fold back under my hand.
Miles of yellow wheat bend; their leaves
rustle away and wait for the sun and wind.

This day belongs to my uncle. This is his farm.
We have stopped on our journey; when my father says to
we will go on, leaving this paradise, leaving
the family place. We have my father's job.

Like him, I will be strong all of my life.
We are men. If we squint our eyes in the sun
we will see far. I'm ready. It's good, this resolve.
But I will never pet the rabbit again.

William Stafford
Even in Quiet Places

On William Stafford

William Stafford is a long-time favorite of English teachers. Associated for many years with the Northwest, especially Oregon, Stafford—in collections such as *Even in Quiet Places* (Confluence Press, 1997) and *The Darkness Around Us Is Deep* (HarperPerennial, 1994)—gives his readers poems that are simultaneously accessible and profound. Stafford co-authored NCTE's best-selling *Getting the Knack: 20 Poetry Writing Exercises 20* (1992) with Stephen Dunning. He died in 1993.

Around the High School

Listen
or not;
you'll hear
them anyway:
the thumping
bass and
rhythmic
drums
of cars
with men
and boys
in them,
their stereos
turned high,
all circling
the campus
like sleek
vultures
or loud
lions,
blasting out
to each of us
the macho
male's hard
dominance

and lewd
electric
mating
cries.

John Laue
English Journal (February 1993)

Heart Attack

The room is stunned, silent, cold;
No longer noisy, not like before.
All eyes looking shocked, at the door,
All are silent, young and old.

One man screams, his heart explodes,
Another runs, another goes.
A few more fall and I must confess,
All this because I wore a dress!

Charity Koone, 8th grade
Harris County Carver Middle School
Hamilton, Georgia

Moon and Stars

Full July moon hangs
above the ALL STARS scoreboard.
The diamond of dust
Rises player-high as girls round bases.
Smoke climbs the bleachers
from opposing mothers below.
"Come on Hon!" "Come on Sissy!" they coach.
They curse bad calls and bad luck
with caring voices.
Our dreams different and the same
for the players on the field.

Sue Glasco
English Journal (October 1993)

Olga

shoulders broad as vending machines,
born to swim the butterfly.

what are you doing in this frail light,
your husky sneakers steaming on the radiator?

You say you cannot write a poem
    delicate pages of novels shred at your touch,
    the floor vibrates
    as you trudge to the pencil sharpener
You will not write a poem
    and in your wake
    lead shavings drift to the ground.

Once you wrote about the time Coach riled you.
You snuck into the snack bar after practice,
rammed one arm up the soda machine and with your pen
    the one you will not use to write poems
punched holes in all the cans
when he came for his Pepsi
he got empties for his coins.

You roared, hidden in the gym,
shoulders like wings ablaze with revenge.

Olga, brawny soul,
    butt your head against the white page,
    take us all to China on your back,
Write me a poem.

N. C. Krim
English Journal (March 1992)

Electra

"Don't you like my dress, daddy?" I would say,
twirling,
letting the deep wine color envelop me,
while my chocolate ringlets of hair
flung about in a crazy dance.
"You look just like your mother," he'd reply.
He scooped me up and tossed me
to the sky.
As laughter
my resonant voice echoed,
replenishing the crisp air.
The soft crushed-velvet layers
of the dress pressed against my skin.
And we danced, but then
she walked in the room.

He ran to
her, touching her hair
laughing, dancing with her.
Kissing her, leaving me
to sit alone and play with
my shiny red dress.

Leah Lenk, 12th grade
Clarkston High School, Clarkston, Michigan

Instruction

The coach has taught her how to swing,
run bases, slide, how to throw
to second, flip off her mask for fouls.

Now, on her own, she studies
how to knock the dirt out of her cleats,
hitch up her pants, miss her shoulder
with a stream of spit, bump
her fist into her catcher's mitt,
and stare incredulously at the ump.

Conrad Hilberry
American Sports Poems (Knudson and Swenson, eds.)

Conrad Hilberry's Explanation of "Instruction"

For a while, our youngest daughter played catcher on a soft-ball team. Like the rest of us, she did what she was taught to do—and added a few flourishes of her own. Both halves of the poem are really lists—easing into a couple of rhymes at the end.

how the cookie crumbles
(jane's sweet revenge)

a girl,
a cookie cutter image of her mother,
and every other
woman prisoner of the sex war
rolled out thin by masculine hands,
placed over the fire,
frosted, decorated to meet his
satisfaction,
another insignificant morsel
in the man's world—

Cookie, shake off that crumb!
tell mr. gingerbreadman to run,
run as fast as he can
before he's eaten
by the fox,
the crimson haired vixen with
poised smiling lips,

before he's just another
token pleasure to a
vindicated woman
who has broken his code
and wants to watch him
crumble in mouth watering
weak-kneed hunger.

Danielle Mangano, 12th grade
Papillion-LaVista High School
Papillion, Nebraska

Danielle Mangano's Explanation of "how the cookie crumbles (jane's sweet revenge)"

The experience: As I looked at a girl in one of my classes, I thought that she must look exactly like her mother. The idea of women being cut from the same mold generation after generation struck me. I also thought about repeating the mistakes that our mothers made, the cycle of male dominance and struggle for autonomy. But patterns can be broken. There is power in the position women are relegated to; they can use it to their advantage. In the story of the gingerbread man he is leading everyone else on a wild-goose chase, but I wanted to portray him as running for his life when the tables turn and the woman is in the power position.

Technique: I really just wanted to use the controlling metaphor of the cookie to tie the poem together. I tried to give a sense of running and then slowing down in the ending stanzas.

My Father Mows the Lawn

My father mows the lawn
And makes barbecue,
Drives the car when we're as a family
And writes the big checks, too.

Mother cooks delicious food
Dusting, vacuuming, always cleaning,
Breast-feeding Baby, raising kids—
But most of this is in the past.

Now Father cooks as well as Mom.
Our complex does not require our strong arm
To rake leaves or mow the lawn.
Mother has her own car and mostly only she drives it.

Dad can vacuum too and wash dishes.
Both boys and girls take out the trash,
Vacuum, or go shopping with Dad.
Mom works at a job, too.

The children make their own lunches
And get on the bus before their parents go to work.
At dinner food is reheated from last night
Or frozen food set to thaw in the morning
From long cooking on weekends is eaten.

Women can do work—from astronauts
Engineers, to soldiers—my father's a teacher,
And all the girls in my family want to be doctors.

Roodabeh Samimi, 11th grade
North Carolina School of Science and Mathematics
Durham, North Carolina

Riding the Moon

Brave little girl   conquer your fears
Ride your shadow over the moon
Scream and laugh hideously into
the fan with a jaded voice
Scare them into listening
Make them understand

Brave young lady   light your candle
and pray to your God let the
sunshine melt your cool clean skin
Play dress-up and slip gracefully into
your mother's low heel pumps.

Brave sweet girl   smile at the
unchained male in the lunch line
Show him your soft gentle carefree
spirit   tell a little white lie if you must

Brave cold woman   draw your sword
and duel blinded to the death
Make your "big important" statement
or I should say pretend that
you have one at all

Brave fearless girl   show them
all   make them wonder who
or what you are   leave them guessing.
After all, a lady *always* knows when to leave.

Lindsey J. Blackburn, 12th grade
Norman High School, Norman, Oklahoma

Jenny Says

Jenny wears socks
even in the summer
and her sneakers
are white
like new
and her knees
are never dirty.
She says "please"
all the time. Jenny's
yard has a flower garden
with yellow flowers
you can't pick.

When Jenny bikes
up and down the street
sometimes she stops
and watches
me. If she does, I catch
bugs and watch them run
up and down
and in-between
the silvery
hairs on my arm. Then
I let them climb carefully back
onto a dandelion
growing through a crack.

Jenny says that's
not nice. And,
she says, I'm not nice.

When she does, I wrap a worm
around my finger
and, I say, it's
a magic ring that will
poison who I point it at.

Joseph H. Ball
English Journal (September 1992)

CHAPTER THREE

Body, Mind, and Spirit

Although statistics suggest strongly that Americans are, collectively, unfit and overweight, many of today's adolescents are exceptions to the rule. Somehow they have eluded the couch-potato trap. Teachers see these young people come alive on the playing field, in the art studio, or on stage. Many of them juggle demanding college prep studies, after-school or weekend work, and family life. Others may display great talent outside the classroom yet perform marginally when it comes to book reports and SAT scores.

Through sports, adolescents have a chance to know their bodies well, to understand their limits, to set high goals. Through hobbies ranging from studio art to roller-blading, they find interests and aptitudes that spill over into life in general.

We all know young people whose out-of-class achievements are impossible to ignore. By participating in sports, by discovering a passion for the arts or hobbies, by competing with classmates or with themselves, they reach beyond what is expected, beyond what is normal, and they find themselves stronger, more focused, better able to face their futures.

In literature, one reads of many young men and women who find themselves through sports, the arts, or hobbies. A case in point is Alfred Brooks in Robert Lipsyte's *The Contender*. Alfred boxes after school, and, through contending in the ring, he learns that he can be a contender in life. A similar idea is explored in Chris Lynch's powerful *Shadow Boxer*. What George and Monty need to learn is when to walk away from a fight in order to win a greater battle. (Lynch, who bristles at the notion that he is a "sports novelist," has also penned *Iceman*, a novel that depicts the violence that protagonist Eric brings to ice hockey as a form of revolt against his parents.) Among our suggestions elsewhere in this volume, Walter Dean Myers's *Slam* shows a young man attempting to balance his talent for basketball with his aptitude for photography.

Chris Crutcher's novels—*Chinese Handcuffs* and *Ironman*, among others—feature strong female characters for whom playing sports is a passion. Jennifer Lawless (*Handcuffs*) is a top-notch basketball player facing up to sexual abuse, and Shelly *(Ironman)* sets her sights on becoming an American Gladiator.

Some excellent sports literature is nonfiction, which is more popular among many adolescents than are novels and short stories. These works include Madeleine Blais's *In These Girls, Hope Is a Muscle*, Margot Galt's *Up to the Plate: The All American Girls Professional Baseball League*, and Karen Judson's *Sports and Money: It's a Sellout!* Two-time Tour de France winner Lance Armstrong tells his story in *It's Not about the Bike*.

In other nonfiction, Gary Paulsen's *Father Water, Mother Woods* details the fishing and hunting lore that enriched his youth in northern Minnesota and that provide the natural details of his consistently popular novels *Hatchet, The River*, and *Brian's Winter*. As elsewhere, Paulsen's prose rings true.

The "Body, Mind, and Spirit" section is about more than sports. Among current books dealing with the arts are Allen Say's *The Ink-Keeper's Apprentice* and Martha Southgate's *Another Way to Dance*. The former tells the tale of a boy apprenticed to the famous cartoonist Noro Shinpei. The latter tells of the experiences of two African American girls chosen to participate in a prestigious dance school.

In Karen Hesse's Newbery Medal–winning *Out of the Dust*, Billie Jo is a talented pianist until fire badly injures her hands. In order to make sense of her life and move on, she must endure the pain of playing again. Jeanette Ingold's *Pictures, 1918* relates the experiences of Asia, a high school girl in Texas who is drawn to photography and finds that it may become a life-altering hobby.

Poets we include in "Body, Mind, and Spirit" provide vivid snapshots of how sports, arts, and hobbies contribute to the lives of adolescents. In Valerie Voter Bos's "The Dancer," the experience she conveys is so powerful that she, the dancer, is all but transformed as she performs. Kristen Haver's "Twenty-Five Minutes on the Stairmaster" is more reflective, displaying Kristen's keen eye for the behavior of men and women exercising at an unidentified spa. Others in the collection convey the intense competition of chess (Andrew Shawhan in "An Endless Plane of Squares"), basketball

(Kellen Walter's "The Assist"), and sailing (David M. Darst's "Twenty-Five Knots").

Some of our poets are clearly playing with—having fun with—language. We think you'll enjoy the visual effects of Josh Robinson's "Progression" and Tara Ritchie's "Ski." We certainly did.

Reminiscences

Jim: I wasn't much of an athlete. I remember going out for football in eighth grade. I huffed and puffed around the track as best I could, but the coach told me I could either pick up the pace or get lost. I got lost. I was sort of like Bobbie Marks in Robert Lipsyte's *One Fat Summer*, only he had more grit in the long run. I eventually found myself through music. Back in the mid-fifties, before Sputnik, we could take two music classes rather than more academic classes such as physics or trig. No one worked after school much, so we were able to really immerse ourselves in sports, music . . . whatever.

As a teacher and father, I got a better sense for how much athletics contributes to a young person's development. During my younger son's school years, my wife and I became true "soccer parents"—for twelve years. We must have gone to three or four hundred games. Rogers, our son, put as much into soccer as he did into math and science and editing the school newspaper—and that was plenty.

Dawnelle: I was never much into developing myself athletically. I tried my hand at basketball and soccer in elementary school and found that, number one, the experience didn't thrill me at all and, number two, I just plain wasn't that coordinated. So my sports journey was short-lived. I was, however, very concerned with my body in middle and high school, as were most of my peers. Different parts of me were either too big or too small. Though I longed to look like a "cover girl" early in my teenage years—buying all the right clothes and makeup—I soon accepted that this wasn't going to happen, so I gave up trying.

Looking back, I now see that at some point I must have, on some level, turned to developing my "inner beauty." Like Jim, I absolutely loved music. The first time I attended a Hickory Choral Society performance (a local choral group recommended by my middle school chorus teacher), I can remember having the very real physical sensation of a full heart. This feeling comes back to me every time I hear a beautiful piece of music, whether written by Beethoven or Tracy Chapman. Music is for me what sports is for many athletes: a vehicle for self-understanding and full expression, a coming together of mind and heart.

Poets' Explanations

See Valerie Voter Bos's short essay on why and how she wrote "The Dancer" on page 60. Birmingham poet Charles Ghigna's explanation of his poem "Coach" concludes "Body, Mind, and Spirit."

References

Armstrong, L., with Jenkins, S. (2000). *It's not about the bike*. New York: Putnam.

Blais, M. (1995). *In these girls, hope is a muscle*. New York: Warner.

Crutcher, C. (1989). *Chinese handcuffs*. New York: Greenwillow.

Crutcher, C. (1995). *Ironman: A Novel*. New York: Greenwillow.

Galt, M.(1995). *Up to the plate: The All American Girls Professional Baseball League*. Minneapolis: Lerner.

Hesse, K. (1997). *Out of the dust*. New York: Scholastic.

Ingold, J. (1998). *Pictures, 1918*. New York: Puffin.

Judson, K. (1995). *Sports and money: It's a sellout!* Springfield, NJ: Enslow.

Lipsyte, R. (1967). *The contender*. New York: Harper & Row.

Lipsyte, R. (1991). *One fat summer*. New York: HarperKeypoint.

Lynch, C. (1994). *Iceman*. New York: HarperCollins.

Lynch, C. (1993). *Shadow boxer*. New York: HarperCollins.

Myers, W. D. (1996). *Slam!* New York: Scholastic.

Paulsen, G. (1987). *Hatchet*. New York: Bradbury.

Paulsen, G. (1991). *The river*. New York: Delacorte.

Paulsen, G. (1996). *Brian's winter*. New York: Delacorte.

Paulsen, G. (1996). *Father water, mother woods: Essays on hunting and fishing in the North Woods*. New York: Bantam Doubleday Dell. (Original work published 1994)

Say, A. (1994). *The ink-keeper's apprentice*. Boston: Houghton Mifflin. (Original work published 1979)

Southgate, M. (1996). *Another way to dance*. New York: Delacorte.

The Dancer

Intense breathing
muscles tighten as the curtain rises
Can she do it?
Yes, the familiar feeling
builds within her until
it explodes from hcr soul
becoming one with
the lights,
    the music,
        the dance.
No longer aware of her audience is she;
This movement is her own,
until . . .
startled,
she is brought back to reality
by applause . . .
for her.

Valerie Voter Bos, 11th grade
Hardaway High School, Columbus, Georgia

Valerie Voter Bos's Explanation of "The Dancer"

Experience: The poem's meaning is two-fold: on one level, it refers to amateur (and professional!) artists who experience moments of self-doubt prior to the curtain's rising. I would rehearse steps in my head constantly before the performance, all the while worrying my mind would blank before the audience's careful eyes and ears. On the second and deeper level, the poem reflects my experience during performances. I later realized I would not become the professional I longed to be. But the momentum and passion I felt onstage would always be mine, as well as the applause.

Technique: The poem reflects the "out of body" feeling; it's written in third person about myself. The physical shape reflects the movement and fluidity she exudes. The first ellipsis demonstrates an abrupt interruption as the applause reminds her where she is; the second shows a happy realization, this time at the end of her performance.

Twenty-Five Minutes on the Stairmaster

Twenty more:
A granny on the bike for five minutes reading *Redbook*.
Her hair is short and permed in a grey nest held together by
    hairspray and bobby pins.
She wears golden tennis shoes and a silver jumpsuit.
She leaves after the bike.

Fifteen more:
Old men in tight shirts walk on the treadmill, their beer bellies
    quaking with each strenuous step.
They're spandex outcasts forced to retreat into large and faded,
    double oversized, sweats.

Ten more:

Ripped, red-headed lady's man, do you think you could walk
    past that mirror one more time?

He runs his fingers through his hair, smoothing down the
    misplaced strands with his palm.

He glares into your eyes, gives a pouty smile to show everyone
    that he's buff, and knows it.

Five more:

Tiny, tight-butt blonde slinking around in leopard skin leo-
    tards; prowling for a date on Friday.

She casually walks up to each sweaty twenty-year-old,

Batting her eyes as she compliments them on how much they
    can lift.

They smile, and flex their muscles as they eagerly spill their
    numbers onto a scrap of paper.

She takes it in hand, gives a smile, and then turns away while
    slipping the note under her bra.

Then moves in for the next kill.

One more:

Girls, barely even women, file into the gym for a full day
    workout.

Trendy, name-brand sweat suits and chilled imported ice water
    fill their bags.

They munch on celery and carrots as they listen to the TV and
    music to ease their minds of the

pain, for they are not thin enough, never thin enough.

Kristen Haver, 12th grade
Hunterdon Central Regional High School
Flemington, New Jersey

Pumping Iron

She doesn't want
the bunchy look
of male lifters:
torso an unyielding love-knot,
arms hard at mid-boil.
Doesn't want
the dancing biceps
of pros.
Just to run her flesh
up the flagpole
of her body,
to pull her roaming flab
into tighter cascades,
machete a waist
through the jungle
of her hips,
a trim waist
two hands might grip
as a bouquet.

Diane Ackerman
Jaguar of Sweet Laughter: New and Selected Poems

Match Point

Poised and waiting for the next shot,
Hands sweating, legs like lead.
I have already laid out my strategic plot,
Stepping forward I attack the ball.
Victorious in the point,
Winning it all.

Jonathan Liebtag, 10th grade
Brookfield High School, Brookfield, Connecticut

Forgotten Rainbow

I miss color.
It has been so long
since I have seen any bright shades of green or blue.

All day I am trapped
within bleak gray walls,
my eyes staring vacantly at blank white pages.

At home I'm surrounded
by color I cannot see.
My vision's locked in dull textbooks, bored by unchanging
    print.

Sheets of music
stand dusty, neglected,
a promise of vibrant hues I've forgotten how to call forth.

How can music
have strains of color,
when the musician sees only black and white?

I long to look
around and absorb
the sweet, rich shades of the world.

I know there's a rainbow,
for it glimmers,
tantalizing, just out of sight.

Kristen MacGorman, 10th grade
Norman High School, Norman, Oklahoma

The Runner

Off the couch
onto the floor
through the kitchen
out the door
down the street
over the bridge
under the highway
through the woods
and back again
he takes his morning run

Chris Gibbs, 6th grade
River Oaks Baptist School
Houston, Texas

Twenty-Five Knots

Hands frozen into claws
Grip the taut lines
While shoulders ache
With unaccustomed pain.

Feet seek a secure perch
As heads whip low
To miss the boom
And sails dance their response.

Waves greet the submerged rail
With a harsh slap
That no one hears
Lost in thoughts beyond reach.

David M. Darst Jr., 10th grade
Brunswick School, Greenwich
Connecticut

An Endless Plane of Squares

Chess
a game of absolutes
hot-blooded exultation
and cold blooded calculation
ebony and ivory
battling across the board
pawn gambit in motion
slays a bishop
slayer is slain by a knight
who is slain by another
lowly pawn
battle is joined
across the 8 by 8
Slam! Punch in the timeclock
Slash! Opponent's in check
FWOOSH! King flees to safety
quick as the wind
Checkmate!
it is the end
battling endlessly
without end
across the plain
of squares

Andrew Shawhan, 6th grade
Bethlehem Central Middle School
Delmar, New York

Bowling

As I walk into the alley.
I am surrounded by the sweet smell
of highly concentrated tobacco,
the sounds of balls rocketing
down the lanes,
the cheers of drunken middle-aged onlookers.
I place the old and soiled shoes on my feet.
They feel cold and awkward,
like sitting on a public toilet,
Choosing my weapon,
I select a blue spherical object,
known to the layman as a bowling ball.
The ball shines and glistens
under the bright lights of the alley.
I step up to the lane,
two boards to the left,
to make up for my monster hook.
As I fire the ball at my target,
my mind fills with excitement and anticipation.
Crash! Pins flying everywhere.
Just the first step in my conquest of a 300 game.

Josh Sommers, 12th grade
Clarkston High School, Clarkston, Michigan

A Little More

I tie my shoes tight
I stretch out
I get ready
I go a little faster every day
I go a little more
when I'm finished
I want to fall down

I gasp for air
I feel sick
    But I love it
        So the next day
  I get up
      I tie my shoes tight
        I stretch out
         I get ready
   and I run a little more

Emily Tancer, 6th grade
University Liggett School
Grosse Pointe Woods, Michigan

Ski

   Swish
      Slice
         Fast
      Slow
   Spray
Cold
   Windy
      Icy
         Slip
    Slide
   Up
  Down
   Smooth
      Cut
        Turn
          Ski!

Tara Ritchie, 7th grade
Redlands Middle School
Grand Junction, Colorado

The Assist

Point guard dribbles down the court
As if he were John Stockton
The basketball is thrown to an
Open player.
The point guard's hands are thrust open
like the opening of gates, as his fingers follow
through with the pass
The chest pass, his favorite pass.

His eyes focus only on the path of the
basketball
The pass is caught, but in slow motion
Because it seemed like the perfect pass.
Now the center pump fakes and drives the lane
And with a flick of a wrist
point guard has an assist.

Kellen Walter, 7th grade
Redlands Middle School, Grand Junction, Colorado

Start to Finish

I stood in the start.
While looking over the
wand, at the course
I thought about my
goals, dreams, hard work,
ambitions, struggles and
accomplishments.
Knowing that this was my
last trip down a race course,
tears filled my eyes.
I looked to the side to see
all of my teammates and

friends—my rivals—
cheering for me.
Knowing my struggles, they wanted me to
succeed as much as I did.
In 38.4 seconds, it would
all be over. I will
Stand in the finish.

Laura Pope, 12th grade
Clarkston High School, Clarkston, Michigan

Progression

Boy,
 Glove,
   Bat,
    Ball,
Uniform,
  Coach,
    Fans,
Stadium,
  Hot Dogs,
     Popcorn,
Opponent,
   Scoreboard,
      Field,
Plate,
  Pitcher,
Swing,
  Cut,
Man.

Josh Robinson, 11th grade
Southeast Whitfield High School
Dalton, Georgia

Coach

All coaches come from the same mother,
all mothers themselves deep inside.
It is unwritten that they all call you
by your last name, mispronouncing it
as a joke for the seasoned jocks, the chosen few
who learn to laugh and sweat on cue.
Smythe and Schmidt, ha ha, he says are Smith.
Jeffeier and Johnstein, ho ho, he says are Jones.

We were all All American in the mouth of our coach,
in the scent of the gym, in the game he called for us.
We moved, lost in those years
inside the nameless t-shirt,
inside the regulation shorts we had to wear,
inside the opened showers we had to take
for coach's eyes and our uncovered guilt.

Twelve years later, going back for a truer look,
we pause behind the door of the grayest gym
and hear him calling names to the bleachers,
hear him taking the practiced laughs
from those who play, and learn.

Charles Ghigna
Speaking in Tongues: New and Selected Poems, 1974–1994

Charles Ghigna's Explanation of "Coach"

"Coach" was inspired by one of my high school coaches. He was a stern, no-nonsense kind of guy who had difficulty pronouncing some of our names. Those were the good old days before political correctness and sensitivity training. It was also about the time that the slogan "There is no I in team" became a popular poster. It hung over the entrance to the boys' dressing room along with a big, hand-painted board that read "It's not whether you win or lose, it's how you play the game." We marched in and out under those signs each day during PE, each of us wondering if we looked anything like Marlon Brando in our white, nameless T-shirts. Not sure we learned any real lessons from all that. It did, however, inspire a poem.

I wanted to grab the reader and pull him or her into the poem with a jolt. I also wanted to establish an edgy tone of irony. Thus, I chose to frame my opening sentence with a bit of a paradox and end the poem with that same effect. In an attempt to evoke in my readers a few of their own gray memories of coaches and gyms, I allowed my little narrative in the last two stanzas to unfold a little more lyrically and dramatically than the dry, declarative style of the first stanza.

CHAPTER FOUR

Generations

Teachers would agree that the most important relationships our students have as children and adolescents are with family members—parents, grandparents, brothers and sisters, and others. Of course, the characteristics of family have changed over time, especially in the past twenty years. More young people today live with one parent or in blended stepfamilies than was once the case. Though still a very small minority, same-sex parents are also evident in many schools and communities.

At their best, these new family patterns are a source of love, strength, and stability. They can also be the source of stress and alienation. Popular television shows such as *Judging Amy* dramatize both effects.

As the twenty-first century begins, America's twenty-two million teenagers might be called the "home-alone generation." In most households today, both parents (when there *are* two) work. Latchkey kids are the by-product of this trend. *Newsweek*'s Sharon Begley (2000) reports that, in the United States, kids spend one in five waking hours alone—not with family or friends, not at soccer practice, not at work, but alone (p. 54).

After-school programs and day care are society's ways of dealing with working families—at least in the case of younger children. But such programs don't take the place of someone who loves you at home.

Teachers may choose to introduce adolescents to literature that affirms the role of family members in the lives of young people. Beyond this, however, they may use literature that examines families in crisis—families responding to setbacks from outside the family, and families addressing (or not addressing) internal crises.

A sense of family is a powerful recurring motif in much classic and modern literature. One need only think of John Steinbeck's *The Grapes of Wrath* or Alice Walker's *The Color Purple* or

Carson McCullers's *The Member of the Wedding* to recognize that the need for family, the need to care for and be cared by those who are closest to us by blood or circumstance, is a powerful force for almost everyone.

Among books popular with adolescent readers, Judith Guest's *Ordinary People* portrays how the death of an older brother tests family loyalties. Laurence Yep's *Dragonwings* depicts a Chinese American family in San Francisco at the time of the 1906 earthquake and fire. Gary Soto's nonfiction works (*A Summer Life* and *Living Up the Street: Narrative Recollections*) describe his California childhood and adolescence in a large Hispanic family in sometimes humorous, sometimes moving accounts.

Family is equally important in the novels of Cynthia Voigt (*Homecoming* and *Dicey's Song*, among others), Sharon Bell Mathis (*Teacup Full of Roses*), Ouida Sebestyen *(Words by Heart)*, Walter Dean Myers (*Somewhere in the Darkness),* Katherine Paterson (*Come Sing, Jimmy Jo* and *Jacob Have I Loved*), and Mildred Taylor (*Roll of Thunder, Hear My Cry*). In these novels, parents and other adult family members are well-drawn, rounded characters.

Contributors to our "Generations" section express themselves on a range of family topics and concerns. Sandra Cisneros ("My Wicked Wicked Ways") and Margo Zuffante ("Last Photograph") remind us how our past family experiences, captured in photographs, shape us today. Mary F. Jenkins ("Take Your Elbows Off the Table"), Shannon Iezzi ("It's Only a Tattoo"), and Mandy Glover ("Grandma and Me") point out that in all families there are conflicts—sometimes with parents, sometimes with others. Nancy Gorrell ("Blueberry Pie") and Kelly Boss ("Grandma's Ranch") capture the deep feeling we often hold—forever—about our grandmothers.

Reminiscences

Jim: I was a fortunate kid—two parents, a nice home in the suburbs, grandparents close enough to be part of my life. An only child, I seemed to be the apple of everyone's eye. My grandmother, in particular, taught me that I was capable of anything, and—though I've made many, many mistakes in my life—I think she's the primary source of my optimistic outlook on life. My grandfather and I played chess and went to baseball games (the old Washington Senators) in the summer. With him I saw Ted Williams, Mickey Mantle, and Joe DiMaggio. We both hated the Yankees.

My father taught me the power of forgiveness. When I was sixteen I left the emergency brakes off of the family car, which then rolled down our driveway and across the street into a neighbor's yard. I figured I'd catch hell for my carelessness, but my dad just said he was glad no one was hurt. He was my hero.

Dawnelle: My family situation was a bit different from Jim's. My parents divorced when I was about eight. My younger brother and I lived with my mom and were fortunate enough to visit my dad every other weekend. My mom's transition from marriage to single parenthood was downright tough at times. From her, I learned the power of perseverance and inner strength. She taught me that any obstacle can be overcome.

It's only recently that I've learned about my father's experience of the divorce. He left my mom with most of the possessions and, because he wanted to move to Charlotte (about an hour and a half from me and my brother), he didn't have a job. He said that he was scared and didn't know quite where he'd end up or how he'd make a living. But he did it anyway because he didn't want my brother and me to grow up with an image of parents who argued more than they got along. From him, I learned that love shows up in a lot of ways.

Poets' Explanations

Several contributors to "Generations" have provided brief explanations of why and how they wrote their poems. Mary F. Jenkins's explanation of "Take Your Elbows Off the Table" appears on page 79, and Tara Ritchie's explanation of "Giggle from the Sea" follows on page 85. Finally, Andrea D. Firestone provides insight into the writing of "Everlasting Baggage" on page 91.

References

Begley, S. (2000, May 8). A world of their own. *Newsweek, 135,* 52–56.

Guest, J. (1976). *Ordinary people.* New York: Ballantine.

Mathis, S. B. (1987). *Teacup full of roses.* New York: Viking. (Original work published 1972)

McCullers, C. (1985). *The member of the wedding.* New York: Bantam. (Original work published 1946)

Myers, W. D. (1993). *Somewhere in the darkness.* New York: Scholastic. (Original work published 1992)

Paterson, K. (1980). *Jacob have I loved.* Boston: Crowell.

Paterson, K. (1985). *Come sing, Jimmy Jo.* New York: Dutton.

Sebestyen, O. (1996). *Words by heart.* New York: Bantam Doubleday Dell. (Original work published 1979)

Soto, G. (1991). *A summer life.* New York: Dell. (Original work published 1990)

Soto, G. (1992). *Living up the street: Narrative recollections.* New York: Dell. (Original work published 1985)

Steinbeck, J. (1993). *The grapes of wrath.* New York: Knopf. (Original work published 1939)

Taylor, M. (1976). *Roll of thunder, hear my cry.* New York: Dial.

Voigt, C. (1981). *Homecoming.* New York: Atheneum.

Voigt, C. (1983). *Dicey's song.* New York: Atheneum. (Original work published 1982)

Walker, A. (1996). *The color purple.* New York: Pocket Books. (Original work published 1982)

Yep, L. (1975). *Dragonwings.* New York: HarperTrophy.

Making a Briquette Chimney

We don't talk about the lack
of perfect materials.
We go to work without
blueprint or design.

My father finds a stovepipe
and hammers out the crinks.
I bend a scrap of metal
into a crooked handle.

We use guesswork as we build—
how many holes to drill,
where to place the shelf,
where to attach the handle.

We pop in the rivets
and twist in the screws—
the power drill aching
under the extra strain.

Later, we test our creation.
Huddled over, we watch
the hard, dark remnants
of our burnt past, rekindle.

Philip Venzke
English Journal (September 1991)

It's Only a Tattoo

What, Mom?
What are you talking about?
There's nothing on my back.
That's a stick-on tattoo!
Fine, it's not. I don't care.
The real thing is better anyway.
I wanted to get one, Mom.
Me and Steve went to the Tattoo Convention,
had to pay $12.50 just to get in.
I figured I'd get one while I was already in.
I planned on getting one when I was eighteen anyway.
They didn't care if I didn't have an ID.
I told them I was nineteen. They believed me.
I didn't get it illegally!
Your age is just some stupid number.
What difference does it make?
It was safe! They used clean needles every
time and had plastic bags over their hands.
Steve said that's the way they're supposed to do it.
He already had one done before.
Yeah, and I'd jump off the Empire State Building
if Steve did too.
Well it's a good thing I love it if I'm
going to have it for the rest of my life.
You think I didn't know that when I got it?
I don't care if you don't like it. It's my body.
Why are you still yelling at me, Mom?
It's not going to make this disappear off my back.

Shannon Iezzi, 12th grade
Clarkston High School, Clarkston, Michigan

Take Your Elbows Off the Table

Take your elbows off the table!
Ain't you got no manners?
Mama glared at me,
And I glared back at her,
But I still took my elbows off the table.
    Hush your mouth!
    You talk too much,
    And you're too loud.
    Mama rolled her eyes at me,
    And I rolled mine under at her,
    But I still closed my mouth,
    And watched the silence swallow us.
Hey! Stop that fighting!
Ain't you got no love in your heart?
Mama tore us apart,
Like ripping paper in half.
I fell so hard,
I wished just once I could hit her back,
But something in her eyes said:
Don't be no fool!
    Mama died today,
    I couldn't even cry,
    But I could hear her say:
    Straighten up!
    Act like you've got some pride!
    Stand tall! You ain't got nothing to hide!
And I took my elbows off the table,
Because I knew Mama hadn't really died.

Mary F. Jenkins
Flint River Review (1997)

Mary F. Jenkins's Explanation of "Take Your Elbows Off the Table"

My mother was a woman dedicated to instilling in me proper manners and moral values. Small in stature, but dominating in presence, she used her facial expressions, tonal quality, and choice of words to impress me. While I showed resentment in silence, I was always obedient and respectful.

I wanted to show the character of the woman in this poem as strong and exacting, yet loving and caring. Her method was effective. For even after her death, the barrage of commands and directives were still remembered and obeyed.

Grandma and Me

Your pants are too baggy
I like 'em that way
Your hair is too wild
It's a statement I say

What's the world coming to?
Where did it come from before?
In my day we struggled
Today we struggle more

Kids didn't date until late teens
Kids are having sex before their time
The world is scary out there
I think I'll be just fine

Mandy Glover, 12th grade
Gallatin High School, Warsaw, Kentucky

My Mother

Her thin lips pursed tightly
Turning white with pressure
Her eyes
Batting at the speed of light
Like the wings of a hummingbird
Tension streaks her face

She tries to put up a façade
But she can't hide it
I see it in her eyes
The window to the inner workings of her mind

Let me always remember
    her sacrifices
Let me learn
    from her mistakes
Let me always love
    my mother

Alexa Baz, 10th grade
Greenwich Academy, Greenwich, Connecticut

Grandma's Ranch

I wake up, as the sizzling of bacon fills the air
I look out the window at the new litter of kittens on the porch
They are not used to humans yet and run away when they see us
I sip my orange juice and glance out at the blue jays in the
    birdbath
My grandma and I suit up in our clothes and go out for a walk
Red Dog, her dog, leads the way
On Christmas morning, tissue paper litters the living room
Coffee and bathrobed humans chat around the room
I like to go out to the power wheel
My miniature camouflage jeep
I was the chauffeur driving everyone around
I drive it to the lake and around in the tall grass
My blue jeans always get muddy ankles
The horse barn is old and rusty
It is empty now
I was always gonna put chickens in the chicken room
But it never came up
I hip hop the cattle guard
On my way out to the meadow
The garden outside buzzes with bees
And I dodge them as I run
A for-sale sign is nailed in the yard
And the family moves away

Kelly Boss, 6th grade
River Oaks Baptist School, Houston, Texas

flight

they squeeze me tightly
one more time
before they let me go
with crossed fingers
they hope I will come back

I soar
unhindered by their confining grasp
leaving behind their control
forced upon me
oppressive
their images blur
and their words muffle

moving faster
free to see, to decide
I struggle to make the right turn
but find only confusion
rather than a destination

I cannot travel alone
afraid of the freedom
they reluctantly gave me
lost without their direction
I now yearn for it

I choose their guidance and
return to rest
in their open palms

Saritha Peruri, 12th grade
Lake Forest High School
Lake Forest, Illinois

My Wicked Wicked Ways

This is my father.
See? He is young.
He looks like Errol Flynn.
He is wearing a hat
that tips over one eye,
a suit that fits him good,
and baggy pants.
He is also wearing
those awful shoes,
the two-toned ones
my mother hates.

Here is my mother.
She is not crying.
She cannot look into the lens
because the sun is bright.
The woman,
the one my father knows,
is not here.
She does not come till later.

My mother will get very mad.
Her face will turn red
and she will throw one shoe.
My father will say nothing.
After a while everyone
will forget it.
Years and years will pass.
My mother will stop mentioning it.

This is me she is carrying.
I am a baby.
She does not know
I will turn out bad.

Sandra Cisneros
My Wicked Wicked Ways

On Sandra Cisneros

Sandra Cisneros's *Mango Street* is well known to teachers. This rich novel has as much to offer high school students as it does middle-level readers, where it was among the most-taught novels of the 1990s. Her poetry is equally readable. In addition to *My Wicked Wicked Ways*, we suggest—for young readers—the bilingual *Hairs = Pelitos* (Knopf, 1997) and, for adults and older teens, *Loose Woman: Poems* (Vintage, 1995).

Giggle from the Sea

She lies there like an angel,
her breath measured and slow
You sit there wondering,
if she's going to wake up.

Her skin so soft.
Her hair so fine.
Her smile so sweet,
until she weeps.

Her laugh is like no other,
so innocent, so charming.
Her cry is an endless song,
that goes on forever.

Like a giggle from the sea
or a weep from a tree,
she is a little girl
who cannot be replaced.

A full life ahead of her
a long month behind her,
she goes on learning how
to walk, talk, and love.

Tara Ritchie, 7th grade
Redlands Middle School
Grand Junction, Colorado

Tara Ritchie's Explanation of "Giggle from the Sea"

"Giggle from the Sea" is about my little sister. When she was first born, I was amazed at her every move. I loved to sit and watch her. My mom kept telling me that she will grow up fast, just like I did. I thought that writing about her would be a good way to keep her babyhood in my memory. When my teacher said that we were going to learn how to write poems in class, I knew exactly what I wanted to write about!

We started our poetry unit trying to understand figurative language. I came up with the metaphor "giggle from the sea" to describe my baby sister because she is full of surprises and very joyful. I knew from the beginning that my poem would be mostly about this image. From there, I just started describing what she looks like and how she acts. I decided to put one situation or characteristic in each stanza to keep things separate and draw them out. That's how I got how she looks when she lies still in stanza one, what she looks like in stanza two, how amazing she is in stanza three, and where she's going next in life in stanza four.

Last Photograph

A tall, dark man
Wearing a black
Evening suit
Dark hair shining
Under the lamplight
Is lost, but not forgotten
A little girl
With her pretty white dress
And tiny matching gloves
Looks up at him
With sparkling eyes
That match his own
Stay forever smiling
In a tarnished-gold frame
The man's voice
Once so alive
Is longed
To be remembered
Like a song
Where the melody is lost

Never again the same
When a girl
Loses her first love
Her father
The pain
A scab that won't heal
Must be climbed
And then overcome
As a mountain
Would be
Doggedly, with much struggle
Though,

How can pain be overcome?
When pain lives
In that tarnished-gold frame

Margo Zuffante, 9th grade
Lake Forest High School
Lake Forest, Illinois

J. T.

The phone rings
Again.
How many times
Can it ring
In one night?
Homework questions,
Team directions,
No time to chat.
"It's J. T.," Mom calls.
Now I'm really caught.
What does a four-year-old
Know of pressure?

I stare at unread pages
As his small voice
Whirls on
Like a merry-go-round
That never ends.
I want the music to continue,
But know it must stop.
"Got to go now, J. T."
Regret mingled with relief.
"Just one more thing, David."
What could be so important?
"I love you," that's what.

David M. Darst Jr., 10th grade
Brunswick School, Greenwich, Connecticut

June 2, 1989

In Marrero, Louisiana,
I attended my younger brother's first baseball game.
The sun beat down on our faces
As my mother read the latest *Family* magazine,
Dated June 2, 1989,
And I stroked the worm
Squirming in and out of my fingers.
The mud was smooth and left remnants
Beneath my chewed fingernails.

Suddenly, I heard a scream
And a cry for help,
As my brother collapsed to the ground
With his hands cupping his face.
Within myself, I yearned to experience his pain
And I did.
I felt myself scream as he lay crying on the ground
But no sound erupted.
Was he in the same pain as I?
The connection between us was inevitable.
Seeing him in pain tore apart my soul.

On June 2, 1989,
The game proceeded as planned
As the worm managed to escape.

Courtney Bush, 11th grade
St. Mary's Dominican High School, New Orleans, Louisiana

Little Girl Grown Up

I sit in my bedroom
adjusting my cap.
In the bathroom I can faintly
hear my mother crying.
I walk down the stairs
and stand next to the bathroom door.
My mom walks out tissue in hand and says,
"My little girl is all grown up."
She fixes my gown
and straightens my tassel.
The day has arrived,
the one we've all been waiting for.
I'll walk on that stage
with pride radiating from me,
then look on at my friends
trusting we're onto something great.
Some may fear it,
others may love it,
but all of us are moving on.
We are adults now.
Leaving behind the shell of childhood
like the butterfly
leaves his cocoon.
We are mature and able.
And on this day
the world is ours.

Sarah Hool, 12th grade
Clarkston High School, Clarkston, Michigan

Sitting on the Yellow Pages

Sitting on the yellow pages
I looked to my right at
the grid mirror tiles,
My eyes next to my nose
and my forehead askew.
This cake is for me?
I blew out the four candles
on the red and white cake
that matched my red plaid skirt,
and my family clapped.
What did you wish for, they asked,
but I couldn't tell them.
It was my secret.
I wished to be big.
I wanted to wear heels and lipstick
and to drive cars.
As time passed I noticed
my wish was not coming true.
My mom told me I could only wear
makeup at home
and I was slipping in heels.
No, I was not getting bigger
I realized I would just have to wait.

Myrna Enamorado, 12th grade
St. Mary's Dominican High School
New Orleans, Louisiana

Everlasting Baggage

Last summer I left my sandals at home.
The bottoms of my feet burned on the scorching sand.
The year before I did not pack my film.
I spent five times the regular price for it at a Disney World gift
    shop.
And two summers ago I boarded the bus for summer camp
    without my toothbrush.
I used my candy money to buy a new one.

But it was four years ago that I forgot to say goodbye.

And the pain in my heart cannot peel off
Like an old layer of skin.
I cannot hide in a darkroom
And develop pictures of him that I never took.
And I cannot scrub away the guilt growing on my soul.

If I only remembered.
If I only knew.
If I only kissed him goodbye.

Andrea D. Firestone, 12th grade
Parkway North High School, St. Louis, Missouri

Andrea D. Firestone's Explanation of "Everlasting Baggage"

We were assigned to write a poem about baggage for po-
etry class. I decided to take the baggage theme to an emo-
tional level. Even after four years, I was still having a difficult
time accepting the death of my uncle. I wanted to find a
way to express the guilt I felt for not having the chance to
say goodbye to him, even though I did not know that he
was sick. I wanted to show that while material baggage may
seem important at certain times, it is insignificant in com-
parison to human feelings. ▶

I wanted the first half of the poem to have a light tone in order to show the contrast between physical baggage and the emotional baggage that is described in the last three stanzas. Most lines of each stanza begin in the same way to show that I constantly carry this emotional baggage. The reason for carrying this everlasting baggage is the most significant part of the poem, so I made it stand out by creating a one-line stanza.

Blueberry Pie

It was blueberry pie
and the crust was rolled
and folded and flaked and baked
and the heat of the summer day
blended with the heat of the oven
and grandma as pink as a sunset
kissed my cheek with her soft wet
cheeks and the pie spattered blue ooze
on the oven floor and there was only
blueberry air and she peeked in the oven
and it was cooking and grandma said "good"
"it will be ready soon" and she took a spoon
in one hand and me in the other and we opened
the oven door once more and the hot winds slapped
my face and grandma scraped the viscous blue and handed
me the spoon and the burning blue kissed my lips
and we smiled blue all day.

Nancy Gorrell
English Journal (December 1990)

Part II

Close to Home: Classmates, Friends, and Others

CHAPTER FIVE

School Life

L ife at school means academics—algebra and American history, geometry and gym class, computers and equations. Life at school means places and events—homeroom, pep rallies, parking lots, buses, forgettable lunches in the cafeteria, forgotten lunches left beside the door at home. Life at school means relationships—with new teachers, with old friends, with new acquaintances, with coaches, counselors, and class sponsors. Yet teachers recognize that—beyond academics and events and, yes, even people—a young person's life at school is a search for self-definition, for balance, for inner peace, for values that will serve one well in adulthood.

And—let's not forget that school is also a place to gain recognition, to have fun, and to fall in and out of love. School is a source of pride, boredom, and failure. School is where to connect, or to feel alienation at its most terrible. In a phrase, school is where it's at.

Finally, school is a place for making choices, both small and sometimes momentous. The choices young people make in middle and high school are as immediate as figuring out what to wear tomorrow and how to deal with cliques, and as abstract as setting life goals and taking a stand for what is right. Every day, reports *Newsweek*'s Claudia Kalb (2000), three thousand American adolescents choose to begin smoking; one-third have used marijuana, and a similar proportion qualify as binge drinkers. Though discouraging, these statistics suggest that fewer teens are caught up in these practices than was the case in the mid-1990s (p. 67).

Teachers recognize connections between issues that young people deal with at home and those they face at school: roles, responsibilities, identities, and relationships. The differences lie in the cast of characters—parents, brothers, and sisters at home, and teachers and classmates at school.

Literature, both traditional and contemporary, makes clear the powerful interchange between school and life. Among nonfiction works, Frederick Douglass's *Narrative of the Life of Frederick Douglass, an American Slave* emphasizes the fact that the freedman's place in U.S. society depended on his ability to read and write. As Helen Keller describes in *The Story of My Life,* once her teacher Anne Sullivan helped her break through the barriers of deafness and blindness, Keller wanted above all else to go to school. More recently, Rubin Carter's *The Sixteenth Round,* written in prison and reissued following *The Hurricane,* the 1999 film version starring Denzel Washington, speaks eloquently of the power of education as a social weapon. Gary Paulsen's *Nightjohn*—a work of fiction drawn in general terms from the experiences of many slaves—tells of one man who returned to bondage in order to help other Africans learn to read and write.

Teachers may acquaint their students with novels in which fictional characters regard school—or at least school learning—as a place of discovery and refuge. In Virginia Euwer Wolff's *Make Lemonade,* being serious about school is vital to LaVaughn, a fourteen-year-old who takes an after-school job caring for two small children of a seventeen-year-old single mother. In *Push,* Harlem poet and novelist Sapphire describes how a young girl's experiences at home influence her negative perceptions of school and herself as a learner. To rise above her circumstances, she must turn to school, where she begins to understand her mother's alcoholism, her own pregnancy, and her friendships. Cynthia D. Grant's *The White Horse* extends this theme to a teenage mother and her teacher, who discover the meaning of love and family. John Knowles uses the Devon School in *A Separate Peace* as a backdrop for probing the nature of Gene and Finney's friendship, as well as Gene's guilt for causing his friend's injury and subsequent death.

Other young characters view school as a neutral or even hostile environment, sparking indifference at best, rebellion at worst. Gilly, the feisty twelve-year-old in Katherine Paterson's *The Great Gilly Hopkins,* uses school as an outlet for the anger she feels as she moves from one foster home to another. Though she sees herself as being in conflict with her teachers and administrators, it is clear that getting along at school is fundamental to Gilly's life. It is the only forum she has for developing and demonstrating her tough façade.

The darker side of school life is also dealt with by writers of young adult literature. In *The Chocolate War* it is difficult to tell who is more evil, Archie and his preppy followers or Father Leon. Chris Crutcher's novels (for example, *Running Loose* and *Stotan!*) feature both unprincipled adult characters—teachers, coaches, and principals—and those who make a positive difference in the lives of adolescents.

Paul Zindel's novels—his classic *The Pigman* and the less well known *Pardon Me, You're Stepping on My Eyeball!* come to mind immediately—depict some aspects of school as both laughable and forgettable. Zindel pioneered the character type of the alienated adolescent commentator on the school scene.

The school/home relationship also shows up throughout television and movies. In the teen sitcom *Boy Meets World*, Kevin, a typical adolescent boy, explores his relationships with family, with his friend Shawn, and with his girlfriend through the lessons he learns from Mr. Finney, his social studies teacher. The Saturday morning favorite *Saved by the Bell* shows students of all ages taking on community projects, learning and relearning the value of teamwork through sports, and falling in and out of love relationships, growing as human beings with each experience. And it goes without saying that many classic and recent films—*Dead Poets Society*, for one—take place at school. Even to adolescents who may complain about what goes on there, school is the center of the action.

Given the myriad connections between home and school, it will come as no surprise when we point out that many of the poems in this section interweave academics with other subjects. "Children's Jail" deals with social stratification, as does "My Class—Fifth Grade." "What I Learned in School Today" and "On Wiesel's *Night*" explore how community conditions shape us and, in some cases, leave us scarred. "Why I Write Poetry" acknowledges the power of writing as a way of forging relationships and identity— life experiences developed outside the fifty- or ninety-minute class. A more lighthearted poem, "Shoes," reveals the pervasive fashion consciousness among teenagers, while "The Alien" highlights the teenage battle with difference, confidence, and self-acceptance.

Here, as in our "pop culture" texts, we see how school inevitably mirrors and affects—is part of—society.

Reminiscences

Dawnelle: For me, school was one conversation after another, conversations that propelled me toward discovering who I was and what goals I had in life. I fondly remember taking lunch or after-school time to talk with my teachers about everything from what it means to be a writer to how to solve challenging chemical equations to marriage and relationships. From fourth grade on, I felt as if I were drawn to my teachers, both because they made me feel special and because they provided for me an intellectual stimulation that was lacking in talks with kids my own age. Of course, at the time, my friends thought I was a bit crazy. They couldn't understand why I found talking with, say, our chemistry teacher after school just as fun as attending a Friday night dance. All in all, though, I think I led a pretty balanced teenage life. I was able to have it all—the worries about what to wear and the pursuit of life's deepest questions. School provided a space for me to just be who I was and gave me the confidence to carry out my abilities and personality in the world.

Jim: School was too easy, in a way. I found my niche in music and didn't venture out much beyond its safe boundaries. I took a college-prep program, but so did everyone else, it seemed, since maybe 80 to 90 percent of us went to college. My high school was really big, about 2,700 kids in grades 10 to 12 in a suburb of Washington, D.C.

I wasn't an officer of my class or of any group, and I became right much of a class clown, just enough to be funny to peers but not enough to make my teachers mad. That wasn't always true, but mostly.

Dawnelle was very different, I'd say, from me—more grown-up, more focused. I entered high school as a kid and left it as a bigger kid. I didn't know that at the time, but, during college, my immaturity would catch up with me.

Poet's Explanation

See Lucy DePree's short essay on why and how she wrote her poem "Shoes" on page 104.

References

Carter, R. (1999). *The sixteenth round*. New York: Penguin. (Original work published 1974)

Cormier, R. (1974). *The chocolate war*. New York: Dell.

Crutcher, C. (1983). *Running loose*. New York: Greenwillow.

Crutcher, C. (1988). *Stotan!* New York: Dell. (Original work published 1986)

Douglass, F. (1999). *Narrative of the life of Frederick Douglass, an American slave*. Oxford: Oxford University Press. (Original work published 1845)

Grant, C. D. (1998). *The white horse*. New York: Atheneum.

Kalb, C. (2000, May 8). Unhealthy habits. *Newsweek, 135,* 66–68.

Keller, H. (2000). *The story of my life*. New York: Buccaneer Books. (Original work published 1903)

Knowles, J. (1996). *A separate peace*. New York: Scribner. (Original work published 1959)

Paterson, K. (1987). *The great Gilly Hopkins*. New York: HarperTrophy. (Original work published 1978)

Paulsen, G. (1993). *Nightjohn*. New York: Delacorte.

Sapphire. (1996). *Push: A novel*. New York: Knopf.

Wolff, V. E. (1993). *Make lemonade*. New York: H. Holt.

Zindel, P. (1983). *Pardon me, you're stepping on my eyeball!* New York: Bantam. (Original work published 1976)

Zindel, P. (1983). *The Pigman*. New York: Bantam. (Original work published 1968)

Why I Write Poetry

I was born with words in my mouth,
    Choking on Ys and Ns and Qs.
And whenever I part my lips
I become Winnie the Pooh,
    with a pot of sticky words.
I become a well-loved yarn doll who has seen three centuries,
    memories braided together with strands of woven letters.
I become a candle,
    lighting a room with images bright as a peacock's feathers.
I become the volcano,
    spewing my letters as hot syrupy words
that harden into poems.
I become the sky after a storm,
    dusting my pale letters to reveal a vibrant sunset of words.
I write poetry so that when I am old and crooked
    with twisted lips and rippled skin,
I may tell my great grandchildren
    that I have feasted with grizzlies,
    been loved by giants,
    placed beads of fire in my eyes and shone through the
    darkest night.
I will tell them that
    people have climbed my crusted body to peer into the
    crater of my soul,
    and that I have watched over the entire world at once.
And they will smile and live with shining eyes.

Kaitlyn Gilles, 10th grade
Bow High School, Bow, New Hampshire

Your Head Is Spinning Round and Round

Your head is spinning round and round
You're running in your mind
Your feet don't touch the ground
It's a daily tiring grind

You're yelling at the nosy talker
Stressed from homework you didn't do
You left your book in your locker
What if the teacher calls on you?

You're trying to read a scribbled note
That folded paper in your pocket
You're wondering what your best friend wrote,
Guessing why she wasn't wearing her locket

Your quiz was marked in pen with red
A big fat circled sixty-nine
If the parents see that, you'll be dead
Maybe if they don't you'll be fine

You've been asked if you like so-and-so
For the hundredth time today
You're just friends you say in unison no
Will that stupid rumor ever fade away?

The day's almost over, homework's ahead
A "little while" on the phone
And the siblings and dog must be fed
You fall in bed with a tired moan.

Lochanda Collick, 7th grade
Stephen Decatur Middle School, Berlin, Maryland

What's in a Locker?

tennis shoe,
skateboard (blue),
book report—
overdue;
jacket (red),
cockroach (dead),
sandwich bag,
(week-old bread);
paper—lined,
grade slip—signed,
Oreo,
orange rind,
shorts (outgrown),
saxophone,
bubble gum
Choose Your Own
Adventure (old),
sweatband (gold),
styling mousse—
(super hold);
Twinkie (looks
mouldy), hooks—
everything!
(except books!)

Fran Haraway
English Journal (February 1993)

Shoes

Milling around the hallways
they interact and congregate,
then scuffle and squeak
forming new circles

worn-out lazy scuffed shoes
  uptown fashion bug shoes
    bright white gleaming sneakers
      need-some-cleaning sneakers
        shimmer glitter fancy shoes
          final clearance nasty shoes

dainty (with a smirk) boots
  heavy leather work boots
    shuffling muffling pink shoes
      grimy slimy stink shoes
        nurse-like sturdy walking shoes
          chunky clunky clopping shoes

As each pair spins,
toes pointed in their own direction,
the resounding pitter patter
quickly fades away

Lucy DePree, 12th grade
Lake Forest High School, Lake Forest, Illinois

Lucy DePree's Explanation of "Shoes"

From the time I was in middle school, I have been fascinated with clothing. One of my favorite pastimes is watching people at the mall—after I have been shopped out myself, that is. I like to see what the latest colors are, what styles look good on which body shapes, and how the latest fashions look on real people. Clothing tells a lot about the person inside it, and I often catch myself dreaming about the lifestyles of the people I am drawn to as I sit on the mall bench. Is she married? What kind of job does he have?? Is this all the family, or are they a part of a bigger unit?

At some point, my mall people-watching began to merge with my school experiences, though I had much less time there to really "take things in." I can remember being especially taken with people's shoes, probably because the class change crowds were so great that I literally had to watch the ground to make sure that I didn't step on someone or get stepped on myself. It is amazing how many different ways people find to decorate their feet! I think most adults tend to see teenagers as being made from the same mold, as often revealed in their clothing. But the shoes at my high school present a different view. There were also as many shoes as there were people—or at least it seemed that way. That's why I was inspired to write "Shoes."

In writing the poem, I tried to represent the rhythm of the hall as all of these shoes converge during class changes. The first stanza represents a "calm before the hall storm" through its lines formed evenly with the margins. Not a lot of flair here. But then, beginning with the second stanza, my lines begin to unleash themselves, just as the shoes do once everyone starts to enter the hall. Within those middle stanzas, my consecutive rhyming words—"bright white," "shuffling, muffling," "grimy, slimy," "chunky, clunky"— are intended to resonate with two things: the upbeat energy and the fast-paced nature of high school hall life.

My Class—Fifth Grade

Welfare Joe   pale and slow
    always hungry.

Teacher sneaked Joe   past Principal's rules
past cook's   cool eyes   into a storeroom glut
government milk   peanut-butter
 Joe felt much better.

Keith couldn't   read   wanted a truck
to hit him   dead.
Teacher promised she'd   teach him
Relieved   he leaned against her
        weeping.

Ragged Bob and Jan   classroom squirrels
buried candy   by the swings
stolen from   Safeway   the only way
    they could get friends.

Principal   stopped Joe's meals
didn't like   welfare.
Demoted Keith   too far   behind.
 Called   police   reported   Bob and Jan.

Teacher   left.

Kathleen Iddings
English Journal (February 1994)

Children's Jail

A place of social stratification,
An unfair hierarchy exists, but should not,
A place where morals and values are made or destroyed,
A place where education is thought of as a joke,
Like a jungle, where only the strong or fast survive,
And like the jungle, many don't.
A place where leniency is thought of as appeasement,
A place where intelligence is tested, but not used,
A place, like a zoo, that is full of animals,
Who in the beginning, enjoy it,
In the middle, get bored of it,
And in the end, rebel against it.
This place is school.

Derik Gummesen, 12th grade
Salmon Arm Secondary School, Salmon Arm, British Columbia

A Report

Through research
I found:
a daily verse of
lady . . . or June bugs
a draining curse of
coming . . . or going trails
safety in numbers, alone
the buzz in my head, a drone
the mathematics were an anthem,
with a tattered flag
the writings were a script of consequence
yet to be read
I found
I lost
I won.

Susan Floyd, 12th grade
Clarkston High School, Clarkston, Michigan

A Self-Divided Class

A huge project
Has just been assigned
But half of the class
Have something else on their mind

The mall, the phone
The upcoming dance
They'd run out of class
If they got the chance

But the other half is listening
To the teacher's every word
And on more than one occasion
Take notes on what they've heard

What time it is due
Make sure not to be late
What should be on it
After hour, name, and date

Each half gets it done
In their own unique way
One done weeks in advance
The other on the last day

And then they get their grades
Either they fail or pass
And that's how things go
In this self-divided class

Tina Gupta, 8th grade
East Middle School
Farm Hills, Michigan

Outing

Out the back past buses,
out a gate
we crossed a dry field
chatting in twos and threes
then poked and scratched
along the thick wood's edge.

Three girls giggled with their heads together,
whispering about the smell of leaves.

By the ballfield
the sticker bushes parted,
shallow ruts
led beneath the trees
up the hill.
We gathered wild roses, black-eyed susans,
     ferns and thistles,
lavender
and burrs.

Boys scrambled recklessly ahead.
Some stood like paintings of explorers,
one foot set firm atop a mound of dirt.

Stopping still, we listened for the cheeping
of crickets and the clicking of a leaf
falling through leaves
—not the click of pencils,
no locker slams
or voices in the hall.
We dreaded leaving,
imagined hours on the sun-dappled hillside
watching the leaf showers, counting saplings,
watching birds chase-dance through light and
     shade.

A day of class
without the smell
of heated dust.

Time between bells
without the discipline
of desks.

David Burk
English Journal (March 1992)

Lunchtime at Prien Lake Elementary School

Plastic bags of milk decorate the tables,
their punched-in straws rising out of them like spears flung
    hard into
white whales.
Mashed potatoes.
Rolls.
Recess waits out of the windows;
if we turn our heads toward them, we can see into the future.

I sit alone in second grade,
at a green table.
Before I can eat it,
I must twist the stem off of my apple—
one two three four five six seven eight
—until it pulls off.
I stuff the tough stem into my pocket to later
rip it into tiny pieces as I sit at my desk,
finished with my classwork much too early
to have friends.

Bonny Leah McDonald, 12th grade
Lafayette High School, Lafayette, Louisiana

The Alien

Blank faces stare,
but don't actually look.
The only emotion shown
is disgust in their cold,
hateful eyes.
They wish she would just vanish.
To them she doesn't deserve to live.
She is different from them.

"Why can't they accept me?"
she asks.
"Why am I so alien to them?"

They don't care to answer her.
She doesn't deserve to be answered.
She doesn't deserve a chance to live.
She is different from them.

She begins to believe them.
She believes her thoughts are not important,
her life is not important.

She now knows the answers to her questions,
she doesn't deserve to be accepted,
she is different.

Danielle Kaufman, 7th grade
Manhasset Middle School, Manhasset, New York

Another Average Girl

Outside: A lonely girl reads a book in the library
Inside: She's transported to a deep, dark, frightening cave
Outside: She casually leans back in her chair
Inside: She tenses up as she spots an evil dragon
Outside: People stroll by, not noticing the brave girl
Inside: She pounces on the monster and strikes him, hooray!
Outside: She carelessly turns another page
Inside: She defeats the dragon and proudly stands up in
    triumph
Outside: She quietly whispers, "Yes!" then covers her mouth in
    embarrassment
Inside: She's the center of attention as people circle around her
Outside: The irritated teacher calls her to her
Inside: She's a hero
Outside: She's just an average kid

Jennifer Patterson, 6th grade
River Oaks Baptist School, Houston, Texas

What I Learned in School Today

The shots sliced through the early morning air.
Everyone looked and saw him in a corner over there.
"Who is it?" everyone asked.
It happened so fast, in what seemed like a flash.
"He was my best friend," somebody said.
It seemed so unfair because now his friend was dead.
Another student's life was taken,
it seems like it's some kind of chain they're making.
Other students pray that they're not next,
they make it sound like some evil hex.
What did I learn in school today?
How to be scared and what it means to really pray.

Devan Satterwhite, 6th grade
Harris County Carver Middle School, Hamilton, Georgia

The Bully

I argue a lot, though it isn't really arguing,
It just isn't allowing.

I will not allow the criticism, all the horrible lies
Of those who do not even TRY to realize
That this is so wonderful, not bad like they say.

So they call me a bully, although I know I'm not.
I just don't agree with people I know,
Those who cannot see
The good in every flower, beast, and bee.

I always speak out, I must be heard.
But only my real friends will listen to me.

Someday, I hope, all will hear my words.
Unfortunately, though, I believe,
They will write me off as annoying,
Yet persistent as a bee.

Look for the good and you will find
That the bad is only in your make-believes and lies.

Diana Levy, 7th grade
Hyattsville Middle School, Hyattsville, Maryland

Notes for a Writing Instructor
For Mary

You lead,
I follow.
It's that kind of dance.
The music begins
And, properly positioned,
Carefully correct,
We begin.

You dance from
Memorized diagrams.
I long to move to
Half-remembered dreams
But I am here
Stepping backward
Pressured by your hand
To turn in tightening circles:
It's all wrong.
My head back,
Barely able to speak
The words that don't mean
Anything
to anyone.

This is not the way
It's supposed to be.

The song over,
I bow
In deference to
Your authority.
You incline your head
Slightly
In the direction of
My weakness.
The music fades
The lights go dim
And
I am left alone,
Broken
And entered,
Dancing
No more.

Dan Verner
English Journal (April 1990)

On Wiesel's *Night*

I cannot teach this book. Instead,
I drop copies on their desks,
like bombs on sleeping towns,
and let them read. So do I, again.
The stench rises from the page
and chokes my throat.
The ghosts of burning babies
haunt my eyes.
And that bouncing baton,
that pointer of Death,
stabs me in the heart
as it sends his mother
to the blackening sky.
Nothing is destroyed
the laws of science say,
only changed.
The millions transformed into
precious smoke ride the wind
to fill our lungs and hearts
with their cries.
No, I cannot teach this book.
I simply want the words
to burn their comfortable souls
and leave them scarred for life.

Thomas E. Thornton
English Journal (February 1990)

CHAPTER SIX

Individual/Group/Crowd

Finding my own voice. Standing on my own two feet. Being a part of a group. Being left out. Being myself.

Teachers see young people every day in small and large dramas that arise and, we like to think, are resolved sometime during adolescence. Teachers recognize that the most powerful tension of adolescence may be the dual—frequently contradictory—need to identify with others, especially other teenagers, while simultaneously developing and asserting one's own individuality. We all need to belong. Successful people, both youthful and mature, know how to balance themselves as individuals and as members of a group, whether the group is a circle of friends, a team, a neighborhood gang, or a youth group at church, temple, mosque, or other religious facility.

Maybe I don't fit in and never will. Maybe there's something basic wrong with me.

The need to belong creates in some a powerful sense of isolation. Most teens feel this way from time to time; the result may be depression or mindless copying of the group. The costs of isolation rarely make the evening news, but incidents such as the Columbine High School shooting remind us that the issue is both real and serious.

Literature for adult readers provides many examples of men and women facing difficult choices involving tension between group and personal identity. Modern classics such as George Orwell's *1984* and Aldous Huxley's *Brave New World* present futuristic dystopian worlds in which group identity has supplanted individual human qualities, both good and bad. In these novels, Winston Smith and Bernard Max rebel against aspects of their respective social orders that no one else recognizes, much less questions. In *Romeo and Juliet*, the group labels that doom star-crossed lovers are those of their families. *West Side Story*, the modern adaptation of *Romeo and Juliet*, substitutes ethnic gangs—Puerto Rican Sharks and Polish American Jets—for Capulets and Montagues. Among more recent works, Pat Conroy's *The Lords of Discipline* follows Will McClean, a cadet at a South Carolina military school who becomes aware of violent racial discrimination toward the school's first African American student. To go against the code of the cadet corps—to say nothing of going against his closest friends—is simultaneously an agonizing and liberating action on Will's part.

Teachers can use adolescent literature to help young readers examine their own and others' experiences both in a group and independent of a group—or, on the downside, dominated or consumed by a group. Norma Fox Mazer's *Out of Control* shows how easily, when three male friends just "kid around" with a vulnerable female classmate, a sense of right and wrong may be lost. Similarly, Lois Duncan's *Killing Mr. Griffin* dramatizes how a sensitive teen, wanting to be accepted by the "in" crowd, can be drawn into criminal acts that are grossly out of character. In S. E. Hinton's *The Outsiders*, Ponyboy Curtis develops the insight that the class system at his high school—which is divided into the rival Socs and Greasers—limits what he himself can be. Lois Ruby's *Skin Deep* makes the strong pull of extremist groups somewhat understandable, loathsome as they are. Finally, two novels by Marie G. Lee (*Finding My Voice* and its sequel, *Saying Goodbye*) follow a Korean American girl's journey through high school and into her first year of college; individual and group identity issues are prominent in both books.

In *Slot Machine*, Chris Lynch gives the fitting-in motif a humorous twist; at a three-week summer camp for incoming ninth graders, Elvin Bishop learns that strength may come from creating one's own "slot" rather than trying to fit into one of the slots defined—seemingly arbitrarily—by others.

Echoing the dystopias of Huxley and Orwell is the fictional world of Lois Lowry in her Newbery Award winner *The Giver*. Twelve-year-old Jonas lives in what seems to be an ideal society, but its flaws gradually become apparent. How and why he decides to leave this community in favor of "elsewhere" is a process of discovering the worth of individual human beings, even seriously flawed human beings.

Poems we include in "Individual/Group/Crowd" illustrate the tensions between individuality and group membership. Lindsay Blackburn's "Heartland" relates how, if one "sleeps in," opportunities to assert personal goals and ideals may be lost by default. "The Awakening" by Philip Odango conveys a paradox of sorts: isolation from the normal elements of life, especially other people, coupled with a sense of peaceful solitude. Both Ted Kooser and Jonathan Harrington highlight the isolation in a world where, too often, people are too busy or perhaps too fearful to notice others. The images of Barry Floyd's "Some Things Suburban" suggest a kind of facelessness in those whom he describes: white kids, loud children, police, and older people.

Reminiscences

Jim: I was into Scouting until my midteens. I identified with the guys in my troop. We camped on weekends during the school year and went off for two or three weeks in the summers, even to international jamborees in California and Ontario. My Scouting friends were a mixed group—some talented, some average guys; some studious types, some goof-offs. I was somewhere in the middle, I guess.

One night—maybe it was in eighth grade—about six of us from the neighborhood rode the bus from Arlington into downtown Washington. We went to Ninth Street, where, in the fifties, were a bunch of dives and peep show parlors. I felt very grown up. The other guys were my age or a bit older, and I admired them more than I care to admit. My parents never found out.

I felt lost in high school at first. I needed to find my niche. There were jocks, college-prep types, and a bunch of kids who rode around in souped-up cars. There were sororities and fraternities—and they were very choosy about who became members. I neither smoked nor drank. The wild parties of these groups, everyone presumed, involved a great deal of both.

Once I got "in" with kids in chorus and the orchestra, I felt like I'd come home. That's where my strongest friendships were formed—the ones that lasted well into college and beyond.

Dawnelle: I affiliated with many groups from middle school on. A church youth group, the middle school chorus, the yearbook staff, the Youth Theatre, and the Hickory Choral Society were all part of the mix of crowds that helped shape who I was and where I was going. Of course, except for the church youth group, which was made up in large part of the "popular kids" in my school, I tried to down play my participation in these groups. While I felt a deep- down sense of belonging every time I interacted with people   in these groups, they were not part of the typical teenage group fare.

I've noticed something different in the students that I teach. They want to fit in, and they have the Tommy Hilfiger jeans and braids to prove it. But there is also an overt need to be "different." I remember vividly the day I told Tierra how much she reminds me of her friend Olivia in her strength for standing up for what she believes in. Though I intended the comment to be a compliment for the neat bond that the girls had formed, Tierra met my statement with disdain: "I'm not so like her, Ms. Hyland! I'm my own person!" She wanted to be seen as unique. I never, never wanted that distinction for myself, at least not then.

Poet's Explanation

See page 120 for Barry Floyd's thoughts about why and how he wrote "Some Things Suburban."

References

Conroy, P. (1986). *The lords of discipline*. New York: Bantam. (Original work published 1980)

Duncan, L. (1993). *Killing Mr. Griffin.* New York: Dell. (Original work published 1978)

Hinton, S. E. (1997). *The outsiders.* New York: Puffin. (Original work published 1967)

Huxley, A. (1998). *Brave new world.* New York: HarperPerennial. (Original work published 1932)

Laurents, A. (1965). *West side story.* In P. Werstine and N. Houghton (Eds.), *Romeo and Juliet and West side story.* New York: Dell. (Original work published 1957)

Lee, M. G. (1994). *Finding my voice.* New York: Laurel Leaf.

Lee, M. G. (1994). *Saying goodbye.* New York: Houghton Mifflin.

Lowry, L. (1993). *The giver.* Boston: Houghton Mifflin.

Lynch, C. (1995). *Slot machine.* New York: HarperCollins.

Mazer, N. F. (1993). *Out of control.* New York: Morrow.

Orwell, G. (1990). *1984.* New York: New American Library. (Original work published 1949)

Ruby, L. (1996). *Skin deep.* New York: Point.

Shakespeare, W. (1965). *Romeo and Juliet.* In P. Werstine and N. Houghton (Eds.), *Romeo and Juliet and West side story.* New York: Dell. (Original work published 1597)

Some Things Suburban

White kids smoking green herbs
In a black forest
Sipping Red Dog
Mosquitoes buzzing around their heads

Loud children
Their voices echoing
Through the quiet
Suburban street

Black birds
Perched atop telephone wires
Ruining new cars
As they drive by

Police
Sirens blaring
Rushing frantically
To the donut shop

Old people
On the couch
Watching TV
Snoring

In the morning
Fresh grass is covered
With wet dew
I hate the suburbs
There's never anything to do

Barry Floyd, 11th grade
North Penn High School
Lansdale, Pennsylvania

Barry Floyd's Explanation of "Some Things Suburban"

I've always complained that there is "nothing to do" in my suburban home of Lansdale. Through my eleventh-grade English class, I really started to notice how writers appreciate the small things in life. You know, the stuff that people usually take for granted. I decided to figure out what I could notice and to combine my careful observations with the notion that there's nothing to do. This is where the irony of the last line comes from.

▶

Basically, the structure of my poem is pretty simple. I just wrote things down as I noticed them. So for all you interpreters out there, there's no inherent meaning in the ordering of the stanzas. I created one stanza for each image, challenged myself to represent the images in as few words as possible, threw in the ironic line at the end, and then I had my poem.

Corrupted Soul

I see me,
I see me thin.

I see a part of me shouting,
shouting and wanting to get
out from within.

My eyes are crying,
my heart is dying.

My body is swelling,
my mind is withering.

I live in this body, it is my home.
My soul and I live here, we live
here alone.

You say that I am fat, you say that
I am round.
You say it with your eyes, without
making a sound.

Shannon Parkison, 12th grade
Norman High School
Norman, Oklahoma

Heartland

Growin' up here wasn't always easy
young girls pregnant
boys slick-haired and stupid
You live here all your
life dust blowin' in your
hair looking for a road
that says The Moon.
Deeper water than these
dry flat lands. The day
you graduate drinking
down your expectations
and dreams with a pony keg.
Wiping the last
few drops from your
mouth only to wipe away
aspirations on your dirty Levis.
Sure growin' up here
wasn't always slick as
pie, but you decide to stay
have a few little'uns and get old.
You wake up one morning and
look up across the dirty river
at the horizon and wonder what your
life mighta been like. I slept in.

Lindsey J. Blackburn, 12th grade
Norman High School, Norman, Oklahoma

how things work

today is going to cost a tear
someone'll smile, a baby will laugh
showing its pink gums, teeth budding through
like a chick pokes its head and beak through the side of the egg.
this, too, will happen today, at least twice.
brother, this is really what goes on.
a happy couple will be brought together in holy matrimony
another heartsick couple torn by law.
a future mother, father, grandfather will be born
a child will take its first step, brother, i remember when
you took yours, unsteady, unsure but leaped at the chance
now you have no fear, brother, this is what gives me fear.
a young man will find happiness with a young woman
they hold hands and gaze into each other's eyes
a block of cheese will go rotten, brother
mold will polka-dot its surface like mussels on an ocean rock
a cat will be adopted today, a well-aged dog will be
put to sleep, a grandmother will sleep eternally
a bouquet of roses, carnations, and lilies will lie across her chest
you soon will experience what really goes on, brother, for now
    just
be a child, i tell you this so you aren't shocked, brother, but
    you still
won't understand that this is how things work . . .

(Based on Gary Soto's "How Things Work")

Jaclyn Peterson, 9th grade
Lynbrook High School, San Jose, California

the unplayed taps

We could not stop, We could not cry
We had not time to say good-bye

it broke Our hearts to see You fall
You're more than letters on this wall

the fading of Your still bright light
was cold and strange and just not right

Fate would not let Us honor You
but now it does so now We do

a message from Your army chaps:
We play for You, the unplayed taps

Joseph McGill, 10th grade
Southeast Whitfield High School, Dalton, Georgia

A Slave's Journal Entry

The glamour all shows,
But behind it is hate,
Shown in a confrontation
Which has no victor,
For this continues without an end,
Puzzled but hopeful as to evil's demise,
We put forth what we can to conceal the hate that lies within,
When will it end?
Why does it go on?
None can choose what they are yet we judge like we can,
Land of the free home of the brave,
More like land of the rich home of the slave,
Who denies the right of freedom?
All who think with an oblivious mind.

Daniel Chavez, 7th grade
Vaca Peña Middle School, Vacaville, California

The Awakening

Night falls, and here I lie alone and cold
scared and lonely in my own dark world
remembering lost memories of old
as nighttime splendors begin to unfold.

Gazing above into the moonlit sky,
entwined above me magnificent stars.
A single jar, thousands of fireflies,
flying, waltzing with the moon, high and far.

Cars and streetlights littered about the town;
Mothers calling their children home to eat;
Fathers pulling in without a sound,
And wives and children at the stoop to greet.

Gazing into the sky, not a soft word told.
And quietly, the night turns into gold.

Philip Odango, 9th grade
Granby High School, Norfolk, Virginia

Boarding House

The blind man draws his curtains for the night
And goes to bed, leaving a burning light

Above the bathroom mirror. Through the wall,
He hears the deaf man walking down the hall

In his squeaky shoes to see if there's a light
Under the blind man's door, and all is right.

Ted Kooser
Sure Signs: New and Selected Poems

Traffic

Every morning
I pass you
at the same spot
in front of the bakery,
both of us rushing to work.

How perfectly timed our mornings must be
for our feet
to touch the same crack in the sidewalk
just as the eight o'clock whistle
begins its shrieking.

I try to catch
the look in your eyes
but you always gaze down
as if something shameful
is happening between us.

At night I lie awake
wondering who you are
as the light from the streetlamp outside my window
pours onto the frayed carpet
of my furnished room.

I wonder
if you too
lie awake at night
somewhere across town
thinking of me.

In the morning
I see you get off the bus
as I turn the corner
and we walk toward each other.
It is a ritual between us.

I smell the warm loaves of bread from the bakery
and hear the whistle
as your feet and mine pass each other
and then are lost in the traffic
of our separate lives.

Jonathan Harrington
English Journal (September 1992)

Road Shoulder Mail Boxes

Road shoulder mail boxes
One rusted metal
Bashed in for fun
By night riders
Teenagers
In search of dragons.

One bright yellow
With red flag up
Signaling life inside.

Mary Ellen Kinkead
English Journal (November 1993)

CHAPTER SEVEN

Peers

Throughout adolescence, relations with peers influence so much of a boy's or a girl's sense of identity and values. At this stage in their development, teenagers tend to shift their loyalties and attentions away from the presumed virtues of adults and toward the presumed virtues of their own friends. Those viewed as role models are more likely to be youthful near-adults recognizable to kids by first name, such as the singers Brandy (Norwood), Britney (Spears), and Ricky (Martin), than to be men and women whom adults know well from national affairs, business, or the performing arts. Mom and Dad, it would seem, can't compete.

Developmental psychology teaches us that shifting one's focus from family to peer group is a natural and necessary process, because forming mature relationships with peers relates to other natural and necessary processes such as setting life goals, refining values, and—eventually—selecting a mate or partner. Given the angst that some parents express when this happens, it seems as if they have forgotten their own youth. As a result, they may lose sight of the benefits—the importance—of the peer group. They don't remember the good that results when teenagers come together to form supportive friendships that provide, among other things, different vantage points through which they may both examine and make sense of the world.

The power of peer connections is an important ingredient of much adolescent literature. In Katherine Paterson's *Bridge to Terabithia*, Jess Aarons and Leslie Burke explore the power of dreams, human relationships, loss, and rebirth in a way that only two friends can. Richard Peck's *Remembering the Good Times* follows three teenage friends from seventh grade well into high school; when sixteen-year-old Trav commits suicide, Buck and Kate help each other come to terms with their loss. Brock Cole's

The Goats tells of a reluctant friendship between Howie and Laura, a boy and girl singled out for a cruel summer-camp prank by older teens. In Karen Hesse's historical novel *Letters from Rifka*, Rifka shares the freedom and independence of America with her best friend, who lives in Russia. In Rifka's case, the act of forming strong peer relations enriches her ability to look beyond herself.

Paul Zindel's novels frequently highlight boy/girl friendships that are essentially platonic. In *Pardon Me, You're Stepping on my Eyeball*, teens dealing with family problems become friends and use each other to work on (and work out) other issues. A more recent novel, Suzanne Fisher Staples's *Dangerous Skies*, also focuses on a boy/girl friendship, in this instance one jeopardized by the fact that Buck, the boy, is White, and Tunes, the girl, is African American.

In John Neufeld's longtime favorite *Lisa, Bright and Dark*, good friends try to assist Lisa, a mentally disturbed classmate, when her parents seem oblivious to her emotional problems. The story is narrated by one of Lisa's friends.

Will Hobbs's *Downriver* is a compelling survival story about several teenagers, male and female, forced to rely on one another on a white-water rafting adventure. Survival through cooperation is also depicted by Julian F. Thompson in *The Grounding of Group 6*; the premise of this tongue-in-cheek tale is that a camp exists where parents send their errant teenage sons and daughters to be "grounded" (can you guess what "grounding" means?).

Two more recent novels—Sharon M. Draper's *Tears of a Tiger* (1994) and Sue Ellen Bridgers's *Keeping Christina* (1993)—tell compelling stories of peer relationships set at school. *Tears of a Tiger*—a documentary narrative built out of conversations, PA announcements, and journal entries—follows Andy Jackson as he attempts to rid himself of a sense of overwhelming guilt for causing a friend's death. In *Keeping Christina*, Annie finds herself struggling to keep old friends when a new student enters her life and begins taking over her family and her peer group.

Of course, many children's and adolescent novels deal with the lighter side of peer relationships. The innocent friendships of the early teenage girls in Ann M. Martin's popular Baby-sitter's Club series provide the basis for one sequel after another.

The poems we cluster in this section tap into the full range of adolescent experiences and points of view that one might anticipate. Several of the poems (among them, Kathleen Aguero's "Beating Up Billy Murphy in Fifth Grade" and Emma Halpern's "How Could She Forgive Me?") deal with the cruelty—either physical or psychological—that young people sometimes inflict on one another. Aguero's poem, particularly intense in its unmediated presentation of a bully's voice that is marked by the speaker's continuing feeling of disgust toward her victim, offers teachers a challenging way to open up questions both about bullying and about gender identity. In stark contrast stands Ryan Starbird's "The Bully," which presents the voice of a terrorized third grader.

At the other end of the spectrum, several poems in this section capture the silliness or the joy of good times with good friends (Kristen Propst's "Summer Day Memories" and Kathi Appelt's "Who Would've Thought"), and still others shed light on the tensions of friendship (Sarah Sando's "Linens") and jealousy (Karlie Bryant's "Little Miss Perfect").

Reminiscences

Dawnelle: I never had a big peer group in middle or high school. I was a pretty shy kid, so I kept to the same group of five close friends for several years. We shopped, went to see movies, set each other up with dates, and shared our deepest fears, dreams, and secrets. We always knew exactly what the others were thinking and were there to support one another through the rocky moments of adolescent life.

My experience was in sharp contrast to my brother's. He was three years younger than I, carefree (but not careless), and never at a loss for things to do with a host of different groups of friends. His biggest issue was where to go with whom when he had three or four invitations for hanging out on a Friday night. I have to admit that I was pretty envious of him. But at the same time, I detested the whole clique phenomenon that seemed to characterize middle and high school life up until about eleventh grade. Deep down, I wondered what it would be like to be a part of the popular crowd—or any crowd at all, for that matter. On another level, that seemed to smack against my very nature.

In watching my students interact on various levels, I've decided that adolescence calls us all into the question of what friendship and peer groups really mean, anyway. It is a question worthy of our pursuit.

Jim: My family moved cross-county the summer before I entered junior high school. Luckily, though, my involvement in Scouting helped me avoid the "new kid" feeling. Lots of the guys I camped with on weekends went to the same junior high in south Arlington, Virginia.

In eighth grade, I was beaten up by a tougher, older kid on the way home one day. I can't remember why—chances are it was my big mouth. I wasn't really hurt much, but I still can feel the embarrassment and rage of being held down, flat on my back, helpless.

Until I was a high school junior, I didn't form any close friendships. No one, until then, came close to being my proverbial "best friend." Then everything changed. In history class, I met Neil, a smart, grown-up army brat who'd just arrived in town from Thailand. Before long we were double-dating, singing a mean copycat rendition of Everly Brothers hits (Neil on the tenor line, I on the baritone), and sharing the secrets of our hearts and souls. Our friendship held for better than forty years through college, high school reunions, and raising families in separate worlds—North Carolina for him, Georgia for me. When Neil died early this year, my sense of loss was great, but, in a way, he will always be with me like he was those many years ago.

Poet's Explanation

See page 137 for an explanation by Adrian Pauw on how and why she wrote "Stir the Fire."

References

Bridgers, S. E. (1993). *Keeping Christina*. New York: HarperCollins.

Cole, B. (1987). *The goats*. New York: Farrar, Straus and Giroux.

Draper, S. M. (1994). *Tears of a tiger*. New York: Atheneum.

Hesse, K. (1993). *Letters from Rifka*. New York: Puffin. (Original work published 1992)

Hobbs, W. (1991). *Downriver*. New York: Atheneum.

Neufeld, J. (1987). *Lisa, bright and dark*. New York: Signet. (Original work published 1969)

Paterson, K. (1978). *Bridge to Terabithia*. New York: HarperCollins. (Original work published 1977)

Peck, R. (1986). *Remembering the good times*. New York: Bantam Doubleday Dell. (Original work published 1985)

Staples, S. F. (1996). *Dangerous skies*. New York: Farrar, Straus and Giroux.

Thompson, J. F. (1997). *The grounding of Group 6*. New York: Henry Holt. (Original work published 1983)

Zindel, P. (1983). *Pardon me, you're stepping on my eyeball!* New York: Bantam. (Original work published 1976)

Linens

Linens
Tugging on all sides,
Like a bed sheet pulled taut
By four friends
One wrenching at each corner.
The seams are about to explode,
And I, the seamstress,
Can only stand by and watch
The sacrilege.
Remembering all the work I've put into that
Which keeps my friends warm during the cold winters
Makes me hate them,
As they rip my love apart.
A friendship out of time,
And out of patience to compete
With the animosity endured each day.
I see the decay of companionship
And the waste of so many good years.
Now I stand helpless,
And watch them tear to shreds
What I need,
And what I have worked so long to maintain.

Sarah Sando, 12th grade
North Penn High School, Lansdale, Pennsylvania

How Could She Forgive Me?

How could she forgive me?
After all I did to her?
She's above it more than I, I guess
She was always almost smiling
Sitting in the back
That strange little girl
Always just about to laugh
As if she knew a secret
No one else did
Or cared about
She never talked in school
We joked she took a nap
That strange little girl
Always just about to laugh
We would always tease her
(Her only dress was brown)
We pulled her hair
And stole her books
Her name, we never even asked
That strange little girl
Always just about to laugh
I didn't cry when I was teased
And became "the Jew"
But as they were marching me away
She went to the window and waved
To think, that's what tore my heart in half
That strange little girl
Always just about to laugh

Emma Halpern, 8th grade
Arthur Rann Middle School, Galloway, New Jersey

Together

Adia had walked out
onto the middle of the bridge.
She paused and looked down.
I saw her tear-filled brown eyes
scanning the gray railing in front of her,
and then the highlighted blue water.
The waves were
smacking against each other,
while the boats screamed,
a long high scream.

With her foot she stepped up
onto the gray railing,
all the while looking down.
You could almost hear
the thoughts going through her head.
It was a battle
between good and evil.

I ran to her.
Our eyes met,
and our thoughts collided.
We had a mental war
between what was sensible
and what wasn't.
Finally she stepped off the railing.
Together we walked home.

Katrina Gomez, 9th grade
Clarkston High School, Clarkston, Michigan

Summer Day Memories

In the bright blue sky on a warm afternoon,
Climbing up rough trees.
As you grab for my hand it fits in mine.
Playing in your tree house up in the sky,
Way up there feeling the cool breeze against my blonde hair.
Feeling free no worries at all.
Remembering those days when we were inseparable.
My grandpa asks me if we were married yet.
"No, I am too young," I would reply.
What a silly old man!
Changing weather didn't stop us,
The cool crisp air which made us shiver
Made no difference as we played in the snow.
Building snowmen and digging tunnels was our plan for the day.
Walking inside, the smell of hot chocolate filled the room,
As we took little sips to warm us up.
Watching cartoons. Playing superheroes.
Pretending that we were pirates.
But, one sad day I moved away.
And now I miss those days up in the tree house.

Kristen Propst, 12th grade
Clarkston High School, Clarkston, Michigan

Stir the Fire

Colors blurred that once burned bright
Take my crayons and fill in with red
the drawings of my childhood
That have faded to grey.

Trapped in the past
I can't keep up with
A world spinning forwards.

Play in my games.
Swing down on the rope so high, so high.
Crawl on your belly or Auntie will catch us
Eating her peapods and strawberries
Seasoned with dirt.

Trapped in the past
I can't keep up with
A world spinning forwards.

Strike a match inside you
I'll light your candle so bright, so bright
Let me stir your fire,
Grind the grey ashes of your childhood
Dirty my hands with your memories.

Trapped in the past
I can't keep up with
You spinning away.

Adrian Pauw, 12th grade
Lewis & Clark High School
Spokane, Washington

Adrian Pauw's Explanation of "Stir the Fire"

Much of my extended family lives on Washington's western coast, and my family visits them during summertime. My aunt sells produce at the market, and everyone helps with picking. As kids, my cousins and I would crawl around sneaking strawberries and peapods while the adults sat up at the house. There was also a chestnut tree at the edge of the woods with a rope that we used to swing up into a treehouse.

There are two voices in this poem: the child, and the adult who uses child-like images. I used this device to emphasize the theme in the repeated stanzas. I also wanted this poem to have earthy images, since so much of childhood centers on discovering nature. This is why I chose the setting (a large garden at the edge of a wood) and images such as fire and ash.

Little Miss Perfect

She's pretty
She's rich
And she is just so darn perfect
Perfect grades
Perfect hair
Perfect makeup
Perfect smile
There isn't one thing not perfect about her
She smiles and guys faint
She drops something they run to pick it up
She throws up and they make a line to hold her hair back
It's quite sad actually
because secretly everyone hates her
I should know
I'm her best friend.

Karlie Bryant, 8th grade
Derby Middle School, Birmingham, Michigan

How Different People Talk in Different Ways

Have you ever noticed the ways people talk?
Robert always stutters his words.
John always seems to scream each word.

Danielle and Rachel always are trading gossip.
Samantha will surely lecture you.
Alice won't let you go without an argument.
But if you just want to talk, that is what
Lauren is for.

Jessica Pratt, 5th grade
Robert J. Burch Elementary School, Tyrone, Georgia

Responsibility

With age comes responsibility.
I never asked for it. It just came.
They would walk down the street.
Like they owned it. I never noticed it then
What they were, I was too young.
Then I was thirteen and things changed.
Sometimes the guys at the corners would ask
I always said no.
My Pa said that stuff would kill you
I never got to try.
The way they walked, with the coolness of a tiger
When they passed the people would quiet down.
God, what I would do for that kind of respect!
I had always been the sort of loser type.
I guess that's what motivated me to join them.
With respect came power. Respect!
Before I knew it, I was wearing the matching black.
Then, one night the blues came, we had to scatter.
Everything went dark.
I never got to see the stars again.
I was so stupid. I had no respect.

Nathan Marwell, 7th grade
Hyattsville Middle School, Hyattsville, Maryland

I Would Never Lie to You

nothing is as it seems
the sky is not blue,
it is azure
the earth is flat,
not round
the solar system revolves around us,
not the other way around
the moon is made of cheese
there is a monster living under your bed
money will make you happy
sex is love,
and vice versa
your parents are always right
your teachers are always right
the government is always right
your local school board is always right
people usually do the right thing
murphy's law is for the superstitious
they're not in it for the money
uncle sam needs you
last night was great
and did i forget to mention,
I Would Never Lie to You?

Orion Nessly, 12th grade
North Penn High School
Lansdale, Pennsylvania

The Day Willie Missed the Bus

Giggling in the five a.m. darkness,
we rushed for the school bus,
eighth grade adventurers
ready to travel across civilized plains
to where Chicago's wilds waited.
We piled on, Dale and Connie,
Judy and me packed in back,
shoulders touching already.
Miss Hasting counted heads:
twenty-eight . . . twenty-nine . . .
thirty . . . only one student missing.

Willie was not there.
Slow Willie, the school bully.
Willie the loner.

Miss Hasting took a last look outside.
"It's time," she said
to accompaniment of thirty cheers.
The bus pulled out,
headlights cutting a path toward Chicago,
leaving behind us the empty schoolyard swings
and Willie running into sight now,
arms waving in frenzied pantomime.
I watched his arms drop to his side
as we turned the next corner,
and I never told anyone he was there.

Gene Fehler
English Journal (September 1990)

Who Would've Thought

Latoya Bentson's living room
was actually a launching pad?

It looked like any other living room:
    couch   lamp   LazyBoy
    coffee table   philodendron

'til last Friday night when
Latoya turned the music
s-o-o-o loud
her great great aunt in the picture frame
    rattle-rattle-rattled
s-o-o-o much
her mama grabbed that aunt
and   hurry-hurry-hurried
to the other side of the house
where it was not
s-o-o-o loud

but not me and not Latoya
and not Susie Myers
and not the Alexander twins
with their matching toes and frizzy hair

'cause the
    beat
        beat
            beat

and our
    feet
        feet
            feet

got all tangled up
    beat, beat
        feet
    feet, beat
'til *u-u-u-up* we went right off the floor!

       Yes!

Good thing Latoya's house had a ceiling there
else who knows
    goodness knows!
where we might have gone

        spinning
    spinning   spinning
      spinning

through the
    living air
in Latoya Bentson's
    living room
last
    Friday
      night.

Kathi Appelt
Just People and Other Poems for Young Readers
& Paper/Pen/Poem: A Young Writer's Way to Begin

Final Note

another Monday morning
homeroom gossip, weekly notices
until a girl with swollen eyes
beckons me aside
"I came to tell you first that Andy's dead."

bits and pieces of his final hour
float in blood and myth about the room
the note   the gun   the message
I CAN'T HURT YOU ANY MORE

minds suspended, hearts choked
we grieve the sudden act of an unformed boy
who wrote poetry about medieval kings
skipped class   but won us with his lonely charm

mourners press to the open casket
but his essence is not there   instead
his fingers pluck each note of the funeral hymn
his mouth shapes each syllable in the eulogy
his defiant shoulders mock us as we wonder why
he chose this place   this time
this violent form of selfish peace

enigmatic to the last he turns   smiles
smokes the Lucky Strike his best friend Ed
planted on the newmade grave

Joan Schulz
English Journal (February 1990)

Beating Up Billy Murphy in Fifth Grade

Who knows how it started?
We were the same age, but he was smaller
with wrists you could snap like green beans,
veins that showed blue runners through his skin.
His scalp was something dead beneath his crewcut
and I hated his pipsqueak voice
his hanging around with us girls.

Then somehow he was face down on the pavement,
my fist banging his back.
When my girlfriends pulled me off,
he whined like a toy engine;
I had hurt his sunburn,
I would pay if he went to the doctor.

He was an orphan I thought I should be nice to.
His aunt was sending him to military school.
I was ashamed but still sickened
remembering his soft hands, his thin eyelashes,
the schoolgirl in him.

Kathleen Aguero
The Real Weather

The Bully

I keep low in class
I try not to meet his eyes
I try not to go where he goes
I dodge him all the time

He is big, tall, and mean
He never fights alone
Instead he has friends
Who act like goons
And come running after me

I sure as hell
Will never tell
Because he will come and hunt me down

And it will be worse
than it was before

I'm in third grade
And I'm hiding from the bully.

Ryan Starbird, 6th grade
River Oaks Baptist School, Houston, Texas

CHAPTER EIGHT

Love

*L*ove! What a powerful word! And what a preoccupation in the lives of many adolescents—or maybe everyone. In adolescence, boys and girls become young men and women. Bodies change. The need develops for powerful connections to others—sometimes physical, sometimes not. The need to "connect" comes earlier in the case of some, later in the case of others.

First love, with or without a first sexual experience, can be all but overwhelming. One feels as if no other person will ever bring together all the wonderful qualities of the loved one. Crushes and infatuations—a strong sense of physical attraction—may be seen as "true love—forever."

Teachers observe that, in a sex-laden culture, issues and choices regarding sexual activity confuse many middle school and high school students. They have known too many sexually active peers who, running the risk of sexually transmitted diseases and, in the case of girls, pregnancy, disrupt and sometimes destroy their hope for schooling after graduation.

The drop in the late nineties in teen pregnancy levels suggests that more of today's adolescents postpone sex than was the case a decade ago, instead finding ways of relating to others without engaging in the ultimate expression of love and desire between human beings. Many, even those who might rebel about some forms of adult control, find themselves affirming the values of church and/or family regarding sexual abstinence. In a recent survey, in fact, more than three-fourths of teenagers in a national sample stated that they are "somewhat" or "very" religious ("A World of Their Own," 2000).

Literature—from the Bible to Judy Blume—is replete with lovers, whether star-crossed, sultry, or downright silly. In the Old Testament, King David betrays his kingdom for Bathsheba. Helen's beauty launches "a thousand ships" in the *Iliad*.

Shakespeare gave us not only *Romeo and Juliet*, adolescents whose feuding families doom their love, but also *Antony and Cleopatra*, in which mature lovers turn their backs on their societies because of love, as well as the giddy lovers and fairy queens of *A Midsummer Night's Dream*. Recent film adaptations of Shakespearean love comedies—including *A Midsummer Night's Dream, Love's Labour's Lost,* and *All's Well That Ends Well*—seek to capitalize on the contemporary moviegoer's preoccupation with beautiful young men and women wooing and being wooed, scheming, betraying each another, and reconciling.

Turning to nineteenth-century British literature, teachers may help their students explore love themes in the work of Charles Dickens (*Great Expectations*), the Brontës (Emily's *Wuthering Heights*, Charlotte's *Jane Eyre*) and Jane Austen (*Emma*, among others). *Emma* became the basis for Amy Heckerling's *Clueless*, a 1995 film that updated Austen's story to the teenage social scene in modern-day Beverly Hills.

Twentieth-century American literature also brings to mind memorable lovers. Zora Neale Hurston's *Their Eyes Were Watching God* is far more than a love story, but its descriptions of Janie Crawford's first love as well as her adult love are striking in themselves. F. Scott Fitzgerald's Jay Gatsby is haunted by his love for Daisy Buchanan. Margaret Mitchell's *Gone with the Wind*, while presenting stiff pedagogical challenges in its deployment of racist stereotypes and in its ambivalent and sometimes approving depictions of racist behavior, also features one of Hollywood's most enduring heroines in Scarlett O'Hara, who vows to "never be hungry again" and is equally intent on making the aristocratic and genteel Ashley Wilkes her man, even as she enters into a complex and troubled relationship with Rhett Butler. Ernest Hemingway's *A Farewell to Arms*, in which a wounded American lieutenant and a British nurse fall in love, explores the tenuous nature of love relationships during wartime. Michael Ondaatje's recent novel *The English Patient* and Anthony Minghella's 1996 film version of the same title also explore this subject.

Some high school teachers introduce love themes through two contemporary novels not written for adolescent readers.

Josephine Humphreys's *Rich in Love* is an appealing multi-layered exploration of love through the eyes of seventeen-year-old Lucille Odom. When her mother abandons her husband and family, Lucille pulls the rest of the family together. Along the way, she discovers a great deal about love—parental and filial love, love between siblings, sexual love, and self-love. The second novel, David Guterson's *Snow Falling on Cedars* has also found a solid readership among adolescents. Guterson, a ninth-grade English teacher when he wrote the novel, skillfully develops its poignant love story between a Japanese American girl, Hatsue Miyamoto, and Carl Heine, an Anglo-American boy, who are high school classmates at the beginning of World War II.

Among novels dealing with love and sexuality that are popular with today's teenagers, Judy Blume's *Forever* is perhaps the best known. In this novel, Katherine has her first sexual experience, but she learns that maturity means accepting the fact that love doesn't always (or even frequently) last forever. Two other engaging older books for young readers that address a love theme are Maureen Daly's *Seventeenth Summer* and Paul Zindel's *My Darling, My Hamburger.*

Issues of sexuality are skillfully portrayed in contemporary fiction by Norma Fox Mazer in *Up in Seth's Room* (abstinence) and *Out of Control* (sexual harassment), by Richard Peck in *Are You in the House Alone?* (rape), and by M. E. Kerr in *Deliver Us From Evie* (lesbianism and homophobia). Ericka Tamar's *The Things I Did Last Summer* follows a male teenager's summer project of losing his virginity; Jacqueline Woodson (*I Hadn't Meant to Tell You This*) and James Howe (*The Watcher*) address aspects of sexual abuse. Woodson's *If You Come Softly* is an interracial love story; Miah is an African American, while Ellie, his first love, is Jewish.

Other novelists explore the lighter side of adolescent romance. Two favorably reviewed works from the 1990s are Colin Neenan's *In Your Dreams* and Louise Plummer's *The Unlikely Romance of Kate Bjorkman.* Neenan's novel introduces readers to Hale—in love (he thinks) with his older brother's girlfriend and oblivious to the wonderful girl who has a major crush on him. Louise Plummer's novel, narrated by Kate Bjorkman, has fun with a traditional love triangle (two girls and one boy) and also provides a great deal of insight into the maturing love of older siblings and parents.

Poets whose work we include in this section communicate the full range of emotions of young love. Tiffany Brandy Trawick's "Drawn" captures the magnetic quality of love, while Donald Graves's "The Bark of Love" echoes Jim Brewbaker's fifth-grade puppy love for Dorothy of the blonde curls (see below). Tara Nicole Tonsor's "Damsels and Dragons" is playful, a what-if flight that many who have loved, young and old, will recognize. Others, like Amy Licatovich ("Our Separate Ways") and Holly Bailey ("Kiss") capture a sadness—even bitterness—in love that has gone bad. Jeremy Casey suggests that true love may be what one experiences behind the wheel of a sleekly shaped car. Well now!

Reflecting a mature perspective, Nikki Giovanni ("A Poem of Friendship") reminds us, "We are not lovers / because of the love / we make / but the love / we have."

Reminiscences

Dawnelle: My first boyfriend, Jeff, exemplified the many faces of love. We were brought together in the eighth grade by friends highly committed to our connection. Our initial few weeks together were the classic first love experience. It was a time filled with joy: he made me feel special with gifts, hugs, phone calls, and messages between classes. I wasn't used to the attention, and it felt wonderful. Before long Jeff discovered what was really important to me, and he challenged me to achieve goals I had been putting off. This made me uncomfortable. Jeff was a giant "yes you can" in my life, but I didn't want to hear it. Our heated discussions about potential and possibility certainly didn't look like love, and I didn't realize how giving Jeff was. Looking back, I realize that he was simply being my champion.

I learned a lot about love from that first relationship. First, love can take many forms! Second, love is abundant; Jeff gave unconditionally, and he never ran out. He created love with me every moment. Third, and perhaps most important, when we strip away everything else, love is all we have, and it is critical to being human.

Jim: I remember falling in love with a girl named Dottie when I was in fifth grade. I was a patrol boy, assigned to stand on the corner and help little kids cross the street. Dorothy, who had curly blonde hair, rode by on a blue Schwinn bike each morning. It was all I could do to keep from running out in the street and declaring myself. In junior high, I didn't date. I was scared of the whole idea—and I was interested in other stuff. For the ninth-grade prom, my parents sort of arranged a date with a girl from the Girl Scout troop my mother helped lead. It was okay. One nice thing was that, for PE, we had dance lessons every Friday throughout junior high. This made being around girls—dancing—easier.

In high school, I fell in love "forever"—twice! I'm glad I wasn't sexually active then. I think it would have been harder to sort out my feelings, to get over the fact that both Mary Kay and Gretchen found other guys more attractive.

References

Austen, J. (1996). *Emma.* New York: New American Library. (Original work published 1815)

Blume, J. (1982). *Forever.* New York: Simon & Schuster. (Original work published 1975)

Brontë, C. (1996). *Jane Eyre.* New York: Penguin. (Original work published 1847)

Brontë, E. (1983). *Wuthering heights.* New York: Bantam. (Original work published 1847)

Daly, M. (1986). *Seventeenth summer.* New York: Archway. (Original work published 1942)

Dickens, C. (1997). *Great expectations*. New York: HBJ School. (Original work published 1861)

Fitzgerald, F. S. (1996). *The great Gatsby*. New York: Scribner. (Original work published 1925)

Guterson, D. (1994). *Snow falling on cedars*. New York: Harcourt Brace.

Heckerling, A. (Director & writer). (1995). *Clueless* [Film]. Paramount Pictures.

Hemingway, E. (1997). *A farewell to arms*. New York: Scribner. (Original work published 1929)

Howe, J. (1997). *The watcher*. New York: Atheneum.

Humphreys, J. (1992). *Rich in love*. New York: Penguin. (Original work published 1987)

Hurston, Z. N. (1991). *Their eyes were watching God*. Urbana: University of Illinois Press. (Original work published 1937)

Kerr, M. E. (1995). *Deliver us from Evie*. New York: HarperTrophy. (Original work published 1994)

Mazer, N. F. (1993). *Out of control*. New York: Morrow.

Mazer, N. (1979). *Up in Seth's room*. New York: Dell.

Minghella, A. (Director & writer). (1996). *The English patient* [Film]. Miramax Films.

Mitchell, M. (1996). *Gone with the wind*. New York: Macmillan. (Original work published 1936)

Neenan. C. (1995). *In your dreams*. San Diego: Harcourt Brace.

Ondaatje, M. (1992). *The English patient: A Novel*. New York: Knopf.

Peck, R. (2000). *Are you in the house alone?* New York: Puffin. (Original work published 1976)

Plummer, L. (1995). *The unlikely romance of Kate Bjorkman*. New York: Delacorte.

Tamar, E. (1994). *The things I did last summer*. San Diego: Harcourt Brace.

Woodson, J. (1994). *I hadn't meant to tell you this*. New York: Delacorte.

Woodson, J. (1998). *If you come softly.* New York: Puffin.

A world of their own. (2000, May 8). *Newsweek, 135,* 52–74.

Zindel, P. (1984). *My darling, my hamburger.* New York: Bantam. (Original work published 1969)

Blinded by the Sun

I lift my face to the sun, the warmth so close to me.
I am glowing, because you gave me roses today.
I stretch my hands to the sun's glare, thinking I could almost
    touch it.
You smiled at me yesterday, breaking the chill of the
    air-conditioned hallways.
Outside I feel like I own the sky, the sun shines only for me.
In school you ignore the other girls, I am the one in your arms.
When we walk through the park, I know that if I had a ladder
    I could touch
the lovely, blazing sun.
Today, though, I have sunburn.
And you forgot to call me.
Feeling cold I reach for the comforting sun, but only grasp a
    handful of air.
In science class I heard you found a new girlfriend.
I also heard that the sun is 93 million miles away.

Alison Faucher, 12th grade
North Penn High School, Lansdale, Pennsylvania

Coin Laundry

we adopted a lonely
shopping cart one day: christened
it with two backpacks and
a guitar and it sang
its squeaky happiness
    thump
thud thud thud thud
as we proudly strode behind it,
our back free from strain.

i think of
the future we
conspired: you and i.
the coin laundry
and caffeine injections. the
bankruptcy at a very young
  age.

we didn't concern ourselves
with planning our
classes at university
rather: how to decorate our
dorm, whether "no pets" included
fish,
whether smoking was permitted.

now
i have quit smoking
and you have started.

it seems we have plotted out
our entire lives this year. we
live on a line
between the future
and the present. building
tomorrow
on what we love today.

now everything is
upside-down.
i'm not so sure where we stand
and i miss those shopping
cart days, but
i suppose that i will always
have
    coin-laundry
    and
    bankruptcy
to look forward to.
someday.

Rachel Devenish, 12th grade
Chilliwack Senior Secondary School
Chilliwack, British Columbia

Drawn

Smoke swirls,
and you suffocate me
Flames fight
and I blister
Orange tongues,
with blue core
engulf me

We dance the fateful dance
of moth and flame

Tiffany Brandy Trawick, 12th grade
South Brunswick High School
Monmouth Junction, New Jersey

The Bark of Love

In fifth grade Miss Adams
moves Elisabeth Lindberg's seat
next to mine in the first row.
Even math is enjoyable after that.

I turn to catch her eye,
and linger in my gaze
to launch a dreamy stare.
I don't dare say, "I love you,"
but I hope the doe-eyed
look will do.
When she glances back, I hold
her eyes, locking so tight
she can reel me across
the aisle to her seat.

I decide to speak to her
and send Katie, my emissary,
to arrange a meeting.
We meet by a tall maple tree
on the street
by her big yellow home
with the balcony on top.

We talk about stupid things
while I peel the bark
off the side of the tree
that stands between us.
I peek around the tree, talk,
peel bark, talk again,
until I finally blurt,
"I just want you to know
I love you."
She smiles and says,
"Thank you," and goes
back to her home.

Donald Graves
Baseball, Snakes, and Summer Squash

On Donald Graves

English teachers are best acquainted with Donald Graves
through his widely read *Writing: Teachers and Children at
Work* (Heinemann, 1983) and his influence on Lucy Calkins,
Nancie Atwell, and others. His poetry collection *Baseball,
Snakes, and Summer Squash* is simultaneously whimsical
and true to life, capturing well-crafted memories to share
with good friends.

Damsels and Dragons

i had a dream last night
that i was a damselfly
being chased by a dragonfly
and you,
you were my firefly,

our orange bodies
were surrounded by
translucent turquoise stars

and you,
you chased away the dragon
and saved me.

that's how dreams are supposed to be, right?
my love is supposed to save me,
a damsel in distress,
and destroy the dragon.

but you,
you blew the fire from your own breath.
but you,
you burned a hole through my heart
but you,
you woke me from my living dream

and i forgot how to fly.

Tara Nicole Tonsor, 12th grade
Parkway North High School, St. Louis, Missouri

Our Separate Ways

When evening came,
the vibrant sun went down
purple,
pink,
and orange colors
appeared in the sky.
Walking down the beach
hand in hand
never wanting to let go
Gazing at the seagulls,
flying by the ocean's graceful waves.

Suddenly clouds appeared,
dark,
gray,
and gloomy
Ocean waves grew,
loud and fierce
The beautiful colors were gone.

And we let go,
walking sluggishly
our separate ways.

Amy Licatovich, 9th grade
Clarkston High School
Clarkston, Michigan

One-Sided Love

Daddy loved Mommy, but Mommy ran away.
Wife loved her husband, but he couldn't stay.
Fan loved a movie star whom she never met.
Girlfriend loves boyfriend who doesn't know it yet.
Girl wants a boy to be her valentine.
Best friend loves best friend, but love he won't find.
What should we be thinking of in terms of one-sided love?

A wife gets beaten, but she can't leave.
A husband's cheating while his women grieve.
A boy gets used, but takes her back again.
A heart gets abused but beats for him again.
Listening to music, the singer steals her heart,
but what is the point when they'll always be apart?
There's nothing quite so tough as one-sided love.

A man can't have a woman because he's too old.
A girl won't talk to a boy because he's too cold.
He can't have her because she's his teacher.
She can't have him because he's her preacher.
She's in love, just not with this guy.
We all have our reasons, but we don't know why.
I think we've all had enough of this one-sided love.

Corinne Lampe, 12th grade
Orion High School, Orion, Illinois

Lovesong

me.me.me.me.
you tune
up in order
to focus
on your own eye
Don't you
think
it's funny
that your
woman
is your
momma
that your
best friend
is your
underpaid
shrink
you.you.you.you.
Doesn't sound
quite
as appealing
to your ears
suits me fine.

Lindsey J. Blackburn, 12th grade
Norman High School
Norman, Oklahoma

Love, Such a Wonderful Thing

with my key in the ignition,
it starts.
sleekly shaped from the manufacturer,
it stalls.
after you start the ignition,
the engine is running,
carburetor's jumping,
gasoline pumping.
the sleek design is unbelievable
the wheels turn,
the pistons churn,
the carburetor burns.
you change gears to put it in park,
you choke it again
you shift like it's a sin.
you just can't win.
Love, such a wonderful thing.

Jeremy Casey, 10th grade
Currituck County High School
Barco, North Carolina

A Game

It started with but a glance and grew to stares.
Thoughts running through your brain as you turn your head away.
"Did she see me, does she know?" You look again.
Your eyes connect, transparent lines from pupil to pupil.
Perfect. Then she looks away, shattering the line
in an invisible explosion. You turn your head back to the front,
trying to resist the urge to look again, you lose.
You turn your head in her direction, trying to establish
the transparent line again. As your eyes look in her general
direction, you see that she is already waiting to make the line.
A half smile forms on her lips, and you swing your head back
to the front. You grin to yourself and once again glance over at her.

She is still looking at you with the half smile plastered to her lips. You manage to shoot a smile back, then you turn to the front grinning. The warm fuzzy feeling flows over you, then you jump as the bell rings, telling everyone that the class is over.
You walk towards her, then just as she looks your way, you shift direction and head to your own locker, cursing yourself for being such a wimp. You tell yourself that there is always tomorrow, but be warned, sometimes tomorrow is too late.

Derik Gummesen, 12th grade
Salmon Arm Secondary School, Salmon Arm, British Columbia

I Know

I've never felt the warm caress
    of a kiss.
I've never felt the soft touch
    of a hand in mine.
And I've never had sweet nothings
    whispered in my ear.
But even so,
    I have learned of love.
It is an unconditional
    comfort.
It is a hope
    that continues on through the despair.
And in times of need
    it never stops giving.
I have learned of love,
    and have a longing for it.

David Clark, 12th grade
Papillion-LaVista High School
Papillion, Nebraska

That Kiss

He couldn't explain at all
what it was like
that kiss
the one he gave
accidentally
to the girl on the stairs.
He hadn't meant to kiss her
except he did mean to
sometime
just not exactly then
on the way up the stairs
between history and English.
It was like it wasn't *him* who kissed her
even though he was
the one
then he couldn't explain
anything—
the feeling
the floating
the air rushing by.
All he knew was this:
sometime after the French Revolution
somewhere in the Universe
he found himself in English
before the bell rang
without taking a single step
after that kiss.

Kathi Appelt
Just People and Other Poems for Young Readers
& Paper/Pen/Poem: A Young Writer's Way to Begin

First Kiss

We felt so old,
yet
we were so young.
Standing there alone
the cold wind blowing through my hair.
My lips were numb,
I could barely talk.
Out of the crowd,
he ran towards me then stopped.
I heard them yell, "KISS HER!!"
Eyes wide open,
he leaned in.
In those quick three seconds our lips pressed together,
I felt my life had changed.
Staring into each others eyes,
we pulled away in shock.
My lips tasted like the strawberry sucker he ate after lunch.
We stood there silent
not knowing what to say.
As he pulled me close,
I smelled his cologne,
he whispered, "I'll remember this forever."

Jenny Davis, 12th grade
Clarkston High School, Clarkston, Michigan

Kiss

Icicles kissed the mire,
Stars of the heart kissed the sky,
Butterflies kissed the flower,
Matches kissed the flame,
Your lips kissed the goblet,
My heart kissed the jagged gate.

Holly Bailey, 8th grade
Leon W. Hayes Middle School
Grand Ledge, Michigan

Women

A woman to dream with
A woman to embrace
A woman to smile with
A woman to cuddle
A woman to live with
A woman to love
A woman to die with

Why can't I have just one of these?
I see the happy couples around me
and long inside for a girl of my own.
But I also see the couples in tears
and think inside,
"I'm glad I'm single."

David Clark, 12th grade
Papillion-LaVista High School
Papillion, Nebraska

Housecleaning

i always liked housecleaning
even as a child
i dug straightening
the cabinets
putting new paper on
the shelves
washing the refrigerator
inside out
and unfortunately this habit has
carried over and i find
i must remove you
from my life

Nikki Giovanni
The Women and the Men

Separation

Your absence has gone through me
Like thread through a needle.
Everything I do is stitched with its color.

W. S. Merwin
Selected Poems

A Poem of Friendship

We are not lovers
because of the love
we make
but the love
we have

We are not friends
because of the laughs
we spend
but the tears
we save

I don't want to be near you
for the thoughts we share
but the words we never have
to speak

I will never miss you
because of what we do
but what we are
together

Nikki Giovanni
Love Poems

On Nikki Giovanni

Nikki Giovanni's poetry appeals to kids, appeals to teachers, appeals to just about anyone. A popular speaker at meetings of English teachers, Giovanni, a professor at Virginia Polytechnic Institute and State University, has published many volumes of poetry, among them *The Selected Poems of Nikki Giovanni* (Morrow, 1996) and *Love Poems* (Morrow, 1997). She is the subject of Carol Jago's *Nikki Giovanni in the Classroom* (NCTE, 1999), a work almost as engaging as Giovanni herself.

PART III

A LARGER WORLD: PERSONAL AND PUBLIC ISSUES AND CHOICES

CHAPTER NINE

Choices, Choices, Choices

It has never been easy to be an adolescent—never. Bodies change, minds change, and the society that teens grow up in changes as well. These biological and sociological factors were most certainly in place in 1900 and 1950, and they are undeniable dimensions of the first decade of the twenty-first century as well. But—because it is now so rapid—change itself has changed since the advent of electronic technology, as Alvin Toffler explained thirty years ago in *Future Shock*. Future shock, Toffler argued, is "the premature arrival of the future." If anything, the personal computer and the Internet have made the rate of change of the 1970s and 1980s seem almost leisurely.

Because of this—because the future is here almost before we know it—young people now coming to maturity face choices not only about "old issues" such as smoking, alcohol, illicit drugs, and sex—the same choices their parents had to deal with—but also about new or intensified realities such as Internet pornography, abortion, date rape, and school violence. It is no exaggeration to say that today's adolescents make such choices—choices that may affect the rest of their lives—on an almost daily basis.

Those who study the twenty-two million American teenagers at the turn of the twenty-first century give the adult generation reasons to feel both despair and optimism. Each day, for example, three thousand teenagers begin smoking. One-third of high school seniors report having used marijuana; another third qualify as binge drinkers. Other choices by teens are unlikely to make headlines but are equally worrisome: only one teenager in ten eats recommended amounts of fruits and vegetables, and one in five is overweight. A significant proportion of the other 80 percent—girls in particular—are likely to be on diets, thus running the risk of falling into an eating disorder. As well, only 15 percent of teenagers get the amount of sleep that health officials recommend (Kalb, 2000, p. 66–67).

On the other hand, statistics on sexual activity are encouraging. Data on adolescent sexual activity, pregnancy, and abortion reveal that all three were on the decline during the 1990s. A majority of sexually active teens reported in 1997 that they use condoms, a trend that contrasts with a 1991 finding that far fewer adolescents were using basic birth control devices. Yet the rate of sexually transmitted diseases such as gonorrhea among adolescents exceeds that of Americans between the ages of 20 and 44 ("The Naked Truth," 2000, p. 58–59).

Making choices and living with the consequences—sometimes ennobling, but not always—is a central motif in many works of literature. More often than not, though, the choices facing characters such as Atticus Finch (in Harper Lee's *To Kill a Mockingbird)*, John Proctor (in Arthur Miller's *The Crucible)*, and Sir Thomas More (in Robert Bolt's *A Man for All Seasons)* are adult choices, not adolescent ones. Whether deciding to defend a Black man accused of rape or refusing to publicly swear to untruths in order to save one's own life, these characters deal with issues and societal pressures that rarely if ever affect modern teens. Other well-known works (for example, Sophocles' *Antigone* and George Bernard Shaw's *Saint Joan)* portray younger characters facing ultimate choices, yet—even when, as in these two dramas, the characters are nominally adolescents—they are larger than life, and their worlds are distant from those of today's fourteen- or sixteen-year-old. Still others—Marjorie Kinnan Rawlings's *The Yearling* or Stephen Crane's *The Red Badge of Courage*—present adolescent boys facing terrible choices that are somewhat closer to modern realities but still uncommon for most.

Skillful teachers help teens understand that, although they cannot determine some aspects of their lives, there are many others that they do, in fact, control. When we use literature that helps our students first discover and subsequently assert their ability to choose from desirable and undesirable alternatives, we give them something precious.

Literature written for adolescents is replete with young people making decisions—many times very tough decisions—in familiar or believable situations. We have spoken of *The Chocolate War* elsewhere in this volume, yet to pass over the courageous stand taken by Jerry Renault in this, Robert Cormier's most widely read novel, would be a glaring omission. Cormier reminds readers that standing up for one's beliefs doesn't always lead to a happy ending. Other novels by Cormier (*After the First Death, Tunes for Bears to Dance To*) also examine teenagers facing dilemmas. A choice of a different sort is made by Zachary, a California teen, in Michael Cadnum's *Edge*. At first the boy decides to hunt down and kill the likely suspect who has shot and paralyzed his father in a robbery, but then he reconsiders.

Ouida Sebestyen's *Words by Heart* presents an African American girl making a tough, life-and-death decision. Even when her father Ben is mortally wounded by the son of a poor White farmer, she chooses to save his life, trying to live the tenets of her religious faith. In Colby Rodowsky's *Lucy Peale*, the pregnant title character chooses to leave home rather than allow her father to humiliate her by making her an object lesson for followers of his fundamentalist religion.

A generation ago, many parents of today's teens were saddened by the downward spiral of Alice, the title character of the still-popular, anonymously authored *Go Ask Alice,* as she develops first alcohol dependency, then drug addiction, before dying of an overdose. Sexually promiscuous, Alice lives and dies in a pre-AIDS world. More recent novels address sexual abuse; among the best is Brock Cole's gritty *The Facts Speak for Themselves*, a National Book Award finalist.

Both young people and their teachers will gain a clearer understanding of urban gangs after reading Lynne Ewing's powerful *Party Girl*. Set in California, the novel makes it clear that gang membership may be simultaneously a means of survival on the one hand and a life-threatening affiliation on the other.

In the case of Philip Malloy in Avi's *Nothing but the Truth*, a Newbery honoree, his thoughtless decision to hum the national anthem in class precipitates a series of unintended negative consequences for his English teacher. With guidance, many adolescents come to see that what seems to be, on first reading, a fairly funny situation is in fact potentially tragic.

In a trilogy including *One Fat Summer, Summer Rules,* and *The Summerboy*, Robert Lipsyte follows Bobbie Marks, a teen who takes control of his weight problem one summer, as well as comes to terms with local hoods who delight in hassling summer visitors at a lake resort. The two sequels show a maturing Bobby—still master of his appetite—as he develops leadership as a camp counselor one year and, working as a delivery truck driver, becomes involved in a labor dispute following his first year of college.

Finally, we believe teachers will find two short story collections—Chris Crutcher's *Athletic Shorts* and Don Gallo's *No Easy Answers*—especially useful as they develop teaching units about adolescents making hard decisions. Crutcher's collection includes six stories nominally centered on sports but also depicting teens who are dealing with racism, AIDS, and sexism, among other issues. *No Easy Answers*, which Gallo edited, features stories (penned by Will Weaver, M. E. Kerr, Graham Salisbury, and other familiar authors of fiction for young adults) specifically selected to draw attention to adolescents dealing with tough choices.

The poets whose work we include in "Choices, Choices, Choices" dramatize a substantial range of hard decisions faced by today's adolescents as they progress through middle school and high school. Shannon Barr ("Too Early: Learn to Wait") and Crystal Gossard ("Prom Night") address choices that many or most teens must deal with related to sexual activity; the latter poem conveys in powerful language the phenomenon of date rape. Three poems (Tracy Thompson's "Deadly Party," John Cameron's "Have Fun!" and Desirae Andrabovitch's "The Canadian War") speak to alcohol abuse. On a very different note, Janice Mirikitani's "Recipe" is an intimate character sketch of an Asian American girl who wants "round eyes."

References

Anonymous. (1994). *Go ask Alice*. New York: Simon and Schuster. (Original work published 1971)

Avi. (1993). *Nothing but the truth: A documentary novel*. New York: Avon. (Original work published 1991)

Bolt, R. (1990). *A man for all seasons*. New York: Vintage. (Original work published 1960)

Cadnum, M. (1997). *Edge*. New York: Viking.

Cole, B. (2000). *The facts speak for themselves*. New York: Puffin.

Cormier, R. (1991). *After the first death*. New York: Dell. (Original work published 1979)

Cormier, R. (1991). *The chocolate war*. New York: Dell. (Original work published 1974)

Cormier, R. (1994). *Tunes for bears to dance to*. New York: Dell. (Original work published 1992)

Crane, S. (1999). *The red badge of courage: An episode of the American Civil War*. New York: Ironweed. (Original work published 1895)

Crutcher, C. (1991). *Athletic shorts: Six short stories*. New York: Greenwillow.

Ewing, L. (1998). *Party girl*. New York: Knopf.

Gallo, D. (Ed.). (1997). *No easy answers: Short stories about teenagers making tough choices*. New York: Delacorte.

Kalb, C. (2000, May 8). Unhealthy habits. *Newsweek, 135,* 66–68.

Lee, H. (1999). *To kill a mockingbird*. New York: HarperCollins. (Original work published 1960)

Lipsyte, R. (1981). *Summer rules: A novel*. New York: Harper & Row.

Lipsyte, R. (1982). *The summerboy: A novel*. New York: Harper & Row.

Lipsyte, R. (1991). *One fat summer*. New York: HarperKeypoint.

Miller, A. (1982). *The crucible: A play in four acts*. New York: Penguin. (Original work published 1953)

The naked truth. (2000, May 8). *Newsweek, 135,* 58–59.

Rawlings, M. K. (1986). *The yearling*. New York: Collier. (Original work published 1938)

Rodowsky, C. (1992). *Lucy Peale*. New York: Farrar, Straus and Giroux.

Sebestyen, O. (1996). *Words by heart*. New York: Bantam Doubleday Dell. (Original work published 1979)

Shaw, G. B. (1988). *Saint Joan*. New York: Penguin. (Original work published 1924)

Toffler, A. (1991). *Future shock*. New York: Bantam. (Original work published 1970)

They Call Themselves Gang-Bangers

They call themselves gang-bangers
With their icy cold stare.
All the home boys dress alike;
They think they're the only ones who care.
Fear settles in schools
And in the city.
What the communities turn into
Is a pity.
If you give them a dirty look
Or dress the wrong way
You better watch your back
'Cuz they'll come after you some day.
How can they be so heartless?
How can they not care?
If you're different then they hate you—
Such discrimination isn't fair.
We're all alike, you and me
There's really no difference that you can see.
They need to wake up to reality!

Katie Moon, 10th grade
Sky View High School, Smithfield, Utah

The Bowman's Hand

> *A 15-year-old athlete died of cardiac arrest from a high
> school friend's punch in the chest during a classroom "cuss
> game" popular with students. Witnesses said he
> complimented his opponent on the "good hit" then died.*
> *—The Birmingham News*

The game over, the target rests on the ground;
but the heavy hand of the standing boy

will carry the weight of this dark moment

into the bullseye of memory, into the
corners of every swollen night.
This is the hand that will open and close

too many times before it sleeps,
before it catches that first star,
shines it bright within its praying palm,

puts it back into the black heaven of boyhood.
This is the hand that will shade the eyes
that study the sky for a cloudless past,

the hand that will grip and hold
the burning weight of growing old.
This is the hand that will not rest in peace,

that will not heal the broken arrow,
that will not lose its quiver;
the hand that will shake inside

the hand of too many smiling strangers.
This is the hand that will caress a sleeping son
named after his father's brave young friend,

after the one untouched by time,
untouched by the sharpness of age,
by the point of a pointless game.

Charles Ghigna
Speaking in Tongues: New and Selected Poems, 1974–1994

On Charles Ghigna

Charles Ghigna is better known as a children's poet and prose author than as a poet for mature readers, and his recent titles for young readers include *Animal Trunk: Silly Poems to Read Aloud* (H. N. Abrams, 1999) and *Christmas Is Coming!* (Charlesbridge, 2000). His adult poems are grounded in the wire grass region of Alabama, where he spent his early years. He has served as poetry editor of *English Journal* and poet-in-residence at the Alabama School of Fine Arts.

Sweep Me Clean

In the beginning they helped me escape my problems
They became an overruling enemy
I became like a fiend
I was their feeble prisoner
My body felt disgustingly dirty inside
I needed to be cleaned too often
I attempted to sweep out the dirtiness
Many different brooms were used
I had to replenish myself everyday
My mind seemed to be going astray
Due to the fact that I brushed myself
A very wrong way

Elena Rente, 9th grade
Little Flower Academy
Vancouver, British Columbia

Too Early: Learn to Wait

Two-year-old Marie
Her mom is seventeen
Her father is gone
Mom couldn't wait so she had sex
Marie's suffering is the result

Her mom always said she would never do a thing like this
Yet Marie is here today
Her mom said she would go to college first
Already a high school drop out
She said she was going to be a lawyer
Is a 7-Eleven clerk
Have a house in Beverly Hills 90210
Lives with her mom in a two-room shack
Have her face in a magazine
Can't even afford to buy one

Marie's mom's friend has straight A's
Has a boyfriend who respects her
College applications on their way
Dreams becoming a reality

Marie's mom is worrying about paying for the diapers

Difference between the two
Marie's mom didn't wait
Marie's mom's friend did
Don't have sex until you have fulfilled all your dreams

Shannon Barr, 8th grade
Mesa Middle School, Roswell, New Mexico

Why?

A little girl
With a shattered dream,
She sits in silence,
Stifling a scream.
She tells herself
That it wasn't that bad,
But those rough hands
Didn't belong to her dad.
Even if they had,
She would feel confused;
What had she done
To call for this abuse?
No one heard her pleading cries;
No one saw the tears.
No one was there to save her;
Now she lives with the fears.
She was too young
To give him what he took,
But he didn't care;
He was a crook.
She had hopes for a family,
But those dreams were shattered.
After what was hers was taken,
Nothing else mattered.
He took more than the preciousness of her womanhood,
More than anyone could know;
He took precious things
That she will never show.
She used to be bright and cheerful;
She used to be brave, strong, and free;
She used to be full of joy,
Not filled with misery.
Now each day comes as it will,

And each hour just passes by;
She's now an older girl
Who still wonders why.

Pamela Buttner, 10th grade
Magnolia High School, Magnolia, Texas

Prom Night

As she walked down the spiral staircase she thought this night
    would be her best;
He was down there watching her in her new lace dress;
They walked out the door arm in arm and got into his car;
Then sped into the dark of night headed for the prom;
But he passed the turn that led to school and she sensed
    something was wrong;
And she couldn't help but feel that something dangerous was
    to come;
He told her it was a shortcut that she shouldn't be alarmed;
But still she had a feeling that this night would bring her harm;
Then he started to go faster and she told him to slow down;
But he just went even faster as they got farther out of town;
And about an hour later the car screeched to a stop;
He threw her in the back seat and then he got on top;
She fought and kicked and pushed him away with all her might;
Then jumped out of the convertible and ran into the night;
But she didn't get too far because he was definitely in shape;
She never thought she'd be a victim to anything like rape;
She cried and screamed even though she knew no one else
    could hear;
And she knew it was all over when he put the gun right to her
    ear;
Then the silence of the night was shattered by a deathly sound;
Her young life was over and her body never found

Crystal Gossard, 8th grade
Lakeland Junior High School, Rathdrum, Idaho

Recipe

Round Eyes

Ingredients: scissors, Scotch magic transparent tape,
eyeliner—water based, black.
Optional: false eyelashes.

Cleanse face thoroughly.

For best results, powder entire face, including eyelids.
    (lighter shades suited to total effect desired)

With scissors, cut magic tape 1/16" wide, 3/4"–1/2" long—
depending on length of eyelid.

Stick firmly onto mid-upper eyelid area
    (looking down into hand mirror facilitates finding
    adequate surface)

If using false eyelashes, affix first on lid, folding any
excess lid over the base of eyelash with glue.

Paint black eyeliner on tape and entire lid.

Do not cry.

Janice Mirikitani
Shedding Silence

Deadly Party

You went to a party
You had a drink,
You knew it wasn't right,
What did you think?
You did it all night,
You smoked a joint,
Who were you impressing?
What was your point?
These things are dangerous,
Don't you care?
Or do you actually think,
You have a life to spare?

Tracy Thompson, 9th grade
Towns County High School
Hiawassee, Georgia

Have Fun!

You think you're in love,
you think you'll have fun?
It's the time of your life.
He says he loves you,
He says he'll never leave you.
You won't get hurt, he says . . .
but nine months later,
You have a little one,
He will call you Mommy
and ask, "Where's Daddy?"

John Cameron, 10th grade
Southeast Whitfield High School
Dalton, Georgia

The Canadian War

The sharp, burning taste of the golden liquid
It is my enemy; your friend.
A long green bottle says Canadian Crown.
A sticker near the neck says in typewriter print 1979.
It scares me; it welcomes you.

Bubbling and churning in my stomach
It's corroding my insides away like erosion did to the Grand
    Canyon.
For you it goes down nice and easy, and settles in its rightful
    spot, like a small rock
being thrown into a pond and sinking to the bottom.
It comes back up for me, it doesn't budge for you.

My head hanging over the porcelain, looking into the water
    that has a septic smell.
The smell is what does it; my insides pour out.
I can see everything I ate that day, and it repulses me to think
    that I was so stupid
To drink it straight, or even in the first place.
I feel as if I have no judgment.

Your head will never hang, but if it does,
It won't be over porcelain.
Your head will hang everywhere, because your coordination
    has left you.
You cannot walk straight,
or recite your ABCs.
But you're happier than me, because you're drunk.

The next morning, you're up by the crack of dawn.
I lie in my bed, unable to move because of the throbbing pain
    in my head.
It feels like my heart is in the wrong spot.
I run into the bathroom to throw up anything that's left
And you just go on, acting as if nothing ever happened.
You'll do it again, and again, and again.
I won't.

Desirae Andrabovitch, 9th grade
South Brunswick High School, Monmouth Junction, New Jersey

Girl in the Doorway

first warm weekend in May
east side of Detroit
she stood nose pressed
against the screen
wanting to be out
on the porch with the three men
older brothers and friends
where the loud laughs were
where they sat you on a knee
and gave you a horsey ride
or lifted you by the arms
and swung you out and down
between their legs
but she was too young
only three and was warned
to stay inside
even on this pink day

so she went as close to the porch
as she dared
and so she saw the car stop
by the curb and the man
get out   walk straight
towards the porch and heard
the three firecracker sounds
but not the fourth

my girl   you are   my girl   dead you
are our girl   in this world we
must share your three years
on earth in doorways
and wish that more screens
protect our other children
                    someday

B. C. Butson
English Journal (September 1993)

CHAPTER TEN

Social Issues

Some observers argue that today's adolescents are detached from the pressing social issues of their times. In *The Ambitious Generation*, for example, Barbara Schneider and David Stevenson (1999) assert that today's teens are optimistic and ambitious, yet directionless. Other scholars are tired of what they see as relentless youth bashing. In *The Scapegoat Generation: America's War on Adolescents* (1996) and *Framing Youth: Ten Myths about the Next Generation* (1998), Mike A. Males writes that adolescents provide a convenient scapegoat on which adults may lay the blame—irrationally—for society's problems. Sociologist Males would probably agree with the teenager who wrote to Ann Landers recently to say this: "Today's kids probably know a whole lot more about how the real world works than most generations. We are exposed to many things our parents were shielded from. . . . I think it's time we were given some respect" ("Teen-Ager Protests Attack on Generation," 2000).

Educators should take comfort in some of the good news about the twenty-two million American teenagers they work with at the turn of the millennium. *Newsweek* reports that nearly half of today's teens perform community service on a monthly or more frequent basis (Begley, 2000, p. 55). The expanding role of service-learning in the curriculum of many schools would seem to be tied to this encouraging trend. A relatively high proportion of 1990s teens abstain from sexual activity (due in part, no doubt, to the fact that more than three-fourths of adolescents say religion is important in their lives [Begley, 2000, pp. 55–56]). Finally, today's teenagers are probably more appreciative or at least more tolerant of diversity—in ethnicity and in sexual orientations—than their parents are. More than 5 percent of today's secondary students are of mixed racial heritage, a figure that is higher in states such as California, Florida,

New York, and Texas, and lower in others. Homosexuality is no longer a taboo topic of discussion at school, a factor contributing to greater understanding of a range of lifestyles and sexual orientations among young people.

Teachers who know adolescents well would probably agree with us that efforts to pigeonhole them as either saints or sinners, either public servants or social dropouts, either focused or aimless, are interesting up to a point but foolish if taken too seriously. Adolescents are peer-driven to a great extent, and they are immersed in a culture that shapes their behavior in powerful ways, but they are individuals first. It wasn't a category of young people that committed mayhem at Columbine High School, but two alienated, disturbed boys.

There are many issues in the greater society that deserve and receive the attention of today's teenagers: school violence and the prevalence of zero-tolerance policies (itself a byproduct of school violence); homophobia and related crimes; poverty and homelessness; sexual abuse; urban sprawl; pollution; genetic engineering; the abortion debate; and the list goes on.

Literature is an important window through which to view the issues of a time and place. In the nineteenth century, Harriet Beecher Stowe's *Uncle Tom's Cabin* stiffened the views of Americans in free states about the evils of slavery. Early in the twentieth century, Upton Sinclair (*The Jungle*) and other muckrakers used both fiction and nonfiction to focus the spotlight on an array of ills either caused or exacerbated by industrialism. Rachel Carson's *Silent Spring*, a nonfiction bestseller, did much to alert Americans to the great harm done by agricultural pesticides.

For decades, adolescent literature has offered examples of idealistic young people challenging the status quo, young people who pose the questions "Where does a teenager fit in the fray?" and "What is society willing to contribute to those on the horizons of adulthood?"

Teachers who respond constructively to adolescent idealism may want to use works by Nat Hentoff (*The Day They Came to Arrest the Book*) and John Neufeld (*A Small Civil War*) to focus young readers' attention on school censorship. In each novel, complaints are made about literature assigned in an English classroom—*Huck-*

leberry Finn in the Hentoff novel, *The Grapes of Wrath* in Neufeld's work. Each provides a balanced treatment of an issue that often sparks more heat than light.

Homelessness and poverty amid great wealth are pervasive problems of contemporary America. Teachers will find that Felice Holman's *Slake's Limbo*, published in the 1970s, is an effective novel for introducing these topics. Though Aremis Slake's ability to survive on his own by holing up in the New York subway system stretches an adult's willing suspension of disbelief, the novel's engaging plotline and general readability make it a solid choice for younger teens. Mentioned earlier in this volume, Norma Fox Mazer's *When She Was Good* also depicts a teenager attempting to survive on her own after the death of her abusive parents and her mentally ill older sister. Irene Hunt's *No Promises in the Wind* tells the story of brothers who, during the Depression, leave home and "hit the rails" in order to survive.

Peter Dickinson's *Eva* explores animal organ transplantation and related bioethical issues—with a decided twist. Once readers accept the premise that, in the near future, putting the heart, mind, and soul of a teenage girl into the body of a chimpanzee is a medical possibility, they are captured by a compelling tale in which Eva becomes the Eve of a new race of intelligent beings. Karen Hesse's *The Music of Dolphins* also addresses a contemporary ethical issue in science through the story of Mila, a girl who was at first rescued, then raised for several years, by dolphins. Rescued a second time by the Coast Guard, she is taken against her will to Boston to be studied by well-meaning scientists interested in her language development.

Hesse also shines her light on another environmental issue, the hazards of nuclear power. *Phoenix Rising,* set in the very near future, deals with events following a Chernobyl-style meltdown of a New England nuclear power plant. Readers experience the aftermath of the meltdown through the point of view of thirteen-year-old Nyle. In *The Bomb*, Theodore Taylor tells a very different story dealing with atomic energy. The novel describes the forcible removal of the indigenous people of Bikini Atoll at the close of World War II so that the United States could test nuclear weapons.

Until September 11, 2001, war was far removed from the world of most American adolescents. To most young people, war was something distant, something seen in history books or in newscasts from countries whose names were hard to remember and harder to pronounce.

All this changed on September 11. We have all felt war—what it does, what it means, and how it affects individuals and nations. It seems almost inevitable now that a new sort of war will be in the foreground of our collective consciousness for years to come. Even in this new and uncertain climate, teachers need to recall that today's seventh graders were infants during the early-nineties Gulf War; their grandparents, perhaps, were Vietnam-era veterans. Teachers who want to introduce their students to war as a theme or issue can turn to *Fallen Angels* by Walter Dean Myers, *I Had Seen Castles* by Cynthia Rylant, or *AK*, a frightening novel by Peter Dickinson that follows a child soldier in contemporary Africa.

In harmony with these works of fiction, the poets in this section write candidly about the issues that hit home for them. John Steele ("My Parents Are Ignorance and Hatred") examines the origins of prejudice. Halle Butvin ("Scarecrow") questions how homelessness can exist in a society of abundance. In "Caylor Street," Brandy Ogle depicts the sharp emotion and reality of the street violence that is all too familiar to many communities. Charles Ghigna's "Keeping a Gun in the House" conveys his ambivalence about weapons, and Robert Renshaw's "The Hill" invites readers to reflect on the human and environmental costs of industrial growth. Kay Meier ("Pictures of the World") and Maryann Matera ("The Survivor") question whether we've really grown at all in our social consciousness, given our obvious continued commitment to warfare and mere survival.

Reminiscences

Jim: Mine was a highly political family. We lived just outside Washington, D.C., and my father was on the rise as a conservative labor-relations lobbyist and attorney. We visited the homes of members of Congress, and they and my father were fishing pals. During my senior year we had to choose a candidate to support and then work in his campaign (I recall no female candidates, by the way).

I remember a family vacation when I was eight. In a Deep South city, my parents went to see the sights, but I chose to stay in the car listening to the Democratic National Convention. "Give 'em hell, Harry!" I remember, as well as the Dixiecrats walking out of the convention to form their own party. Would you believe that Strom Thurmond was their firebrand leader?

To me, politics was heady stuff.

At the same time, most social issues washed right over my head as a teenager. The civil rights movement, free speech issues, organized labor, and environmental concerns meant little or nothing to me. Though I may have been more aware than most kids, I was in tune with the usual things: school, sports, and the latest music.

Dawnelle: Looking back to my adolescent years, it is amazing to me how disconnected I really was from the issues pervading my community, nation, and world. I caught glimpses of understanding poverty, war, AIDS, civil rights, and environmental destruction through my health and humanities classes. But they were just that: glimpses. And I am certain that there were more personal experiences of drug usage, drunk driving, racism, and abuse among my classmates than I'd like to think about. But those things just weren't discussed in the conservative community in which I was raised.

It wasn't until college that I really got in touch with a world beyond what I had known. I discovered that I had unconsciously deemed others as "different," but that, in fact, those individuals had much in common with me. I discovered that issues of poverty, civil rights, and environmental concerns were not an anomaly, not simply U.S. issues, but ones that span the globe. And, most profoundly, I discovered that I could (and still can) do something about those issues that call me forth.

Poet's Explanation

See Jim Brewbaker's short essay on why and how he wrote "Graveyard beside Whitesville Road" on page 201.

References

Begley, S. (2000, May 8). A world of their own. *Newsweek, 135*, 53–56.

Carson, R. (1994). *Silent spring*. Boston: Houghton Mifflin. (Original work published 1962)

Dickinson, P. (1990). *Eva*. New York: Dell. (Original work published 1988)

Dickinson, P. (1994). *AK*. New York: Dell. (Original work published 1990)

Hentoff, N. (1983). *The day they came to arrest the book: A novel*. New York: Dell. (Original work published 1982)

Hesse, K. (1995). *Phoenix rising*. New York: Puffin. (Original work published 1994)

Hesse, K. (1996). *The music of dolphins*. New York: Scholastic.

Holman, F. (1986). *Slake's limbo*. New York: Aladdin. (Original work published 1974)

Hunt, I. (1993). *No promises in the wind*. New York: Berkley. (Original work published 1970)

Males, M. A. (1996). *The scapegoat generation: America's war on adolescents*. Monroe, ME: Common Courage Press.

Males, M. A. (1998). *Framing youth: Ten myths about the next generation*. Monroe, ME: Common Courage Press.

Mazer, N. F. (1997). *When she was good*. New York: Scholastic.

Myers, W. D. (1991). *Fallen angels*. New York: Scholastic. (Original work published 1988)

Neufeld, J. (1996). *A small civil war*. New York: Atheneum. (Original work published 1982)

Rylant, C. (1995). *I had seen castles*. New York: Harcourt Brace. (Original work published 1993)

Schneider, B., & Stevenson, D. (1999). *The ambitious generation: America's teenagers, motivated but directionless*. New Haven: Yale University Press.

Sinclair, U. (1981). *The jungle*. New York: Bantam. (Original work published 1906)

Stowe, H. B. (1983). *Uncle Tom's cabin*. New York: Bantam. (Original work published 1852)

Taylor, T. (1995). *The bomb*. New York: Avon.

Teen-ager protests attack on generation. (2000, July 3). *Columbus Ledger-Enquirer*, p. D9.

Breaking the Doll

Cold.

She was always cold *(cradled*
against my heart she deflects
my skin's living heat)—she
refused to be mothered.

Moldered doll, ruined daughter—
she blinks, crack-glass-eyed,
remembers
my pale fingertip-touch
on her perfect painted lashes,
her sour green eyes
loose a silent accusation.

Fragile baby, abandoned in the far cellar corner
—my father's voice (he's leaving for good
this time) loud in the living room.
His broken-glass words cut through
the cellar ceiling. I reach to cover the doll's ears—
my small hands . . . tremble . . .

Cracked porcelain lips curl.
Dead glass eyes stare transfixed.
They see
the sudden shadow

a child's left hand
Descending toward me from behind.

Tiana Murphy, 12th grade
Borah High School, Boise, Idaho

My Parents Are Ignorance and Hatred

My parents are ignorance and hatred
Wherever there is oppression, you will find me
Making people feel small and unwanted is what I do best
I like to see people cry and feel hurt
People use me as a weapon when they are feeling bad themselves
My brother is slavery and my sister is discrimination
My friends are those who live in the past
I live in the hearts of many to this day
People have been fighting to get rid of me for many years
But I can never be killed until there is unity of all people
This is not likely to happen, not while I'm around
I live deep inside all people, somewhere
Regular people like you have me deep down somewhere
Buried inside your soul just waiting to escape
I am fueled by stereotypes and rumors
By stupid accusations and hearsay
Love, trust and unity are my mortal enemies
You cannot see me or hear me
You do not believe I exist in you
Just when you stop believing in me
That is when I am seen
That is when you know I am there
When you are hurt way down inside
When you can't see a better way of solving a problem
I am your last hope, I am the last place you turn to
And I never solve anything, all I do is hurt
All I can do is make things worse
But you cannot stop me, no one can
The only way I can be killed
Is when all stereotypes and rumors and hearsay
Are eliminated and no one has any hate left within them
But that won't happen, not ever
I will always live deep down
In the hearts of all people, now and for all eternity.

John Steele, 8th grade
Radnor Middle School, Wayne, Pennsylvania

Keeping a Gun in the House

It hides in the dresser drawer,
the conscience of my conscience.
I take it out, clean it, cock it,
put all the bullets back.
If it could talk, it would say:
Who are you kidding,
you're not the killing type.
So you were brave that day,
drove all the way to Wylam to get me,
walked right in and put your money down,
waited another week before
you took me for a ride in the country,
learned what I could do to an oil can.
Is it because your father
never let you hold a real one?
Is it because you watched
all those cowboy matinees?
Read all those paperback Westerns?
Voted for a cowboy president?
So put me back in your dresser drawer
under your underwear where I belong.
Go to sleep and stop thinking about me.
If there's any noise in the house tonight,
I'll be right here waiting to show you
how really loud an inside sound can be.

Charles Ghigna
Speaking in Tongues: New and Selected Poems, 1974–1994

Caylor Street

The lightning crashed, the world came down
A shot rang out with a horrible sound
A young girl falls at her boyfriend's feet
Right there on the side of Caylor Street
The boyfriend sinks down to his knees
Silently sobbing, forgetting his needs
Sirens in the distance real the tragedy
Everyone asking Why her? Why me?
There are never any answers.

At the funeral, many came
Life after was not the same
Something changed with the gunshot's pulsing beat
Something happened there on Caylor Street
No one knows why, but all know how
But why did it have to happen now?
That girl is remembered with memories so sweet
as is the day the world changed on Caylor Street.

Brandy Ogle, 11th grade
Southeast High School, Dalton, Georgia

The Survivor

The day grew dark and black
Barren of life, infested with hate
Children with snake eyes and demon features
Throwing stones of animosity
Into a crowd of fear
Into the thoughts of a survivor

Turn your head—it can't be true

Marched like ants in the rain
Tagged and counted
Nameless faces
A child calls desperately
Into the heart of a survivor

Smoke fills the cloudless sky
The sun screams out for mercy
As she watches the destruction below
Tarnished medals of hope
Dangled from the people's throats
Into the hands of a survivor

The final day—the exodus
Leaving the universe behind
Eyes shut tightly in a darkened world
The last breath of faith
Freedom filtered from the air
Into the dreams of a survivor

Maryann Matera, 8th grade
Howell Middle School, Howell, New Jersey

Scarecrow

Bursting with straw,
patched and weathered.
Sad, forlorn eyes,
frazzled hair plastered down with a floppy straw hat.
Pecked and mocked by the crows,
lips cracked and withered, in a permanent frown.
Coat stained with tears, a citizen of the streets.
Wishing that someday
he could fly away from the torment,
or smile a toothless grin
at a mocking stare.
Wrinkled and gray,
age has not been kind.
Simply bolted down in his rank,
and not given a chance.
Could you spare a dime?

Halle Butvin, 11th grade
Strongsville High School, Strongsville, Ohio

Notice

I sit there, staring,
Gazing upon the terrified Americans.

My friend's parents look at me suspiciously,
As though this war made all Japanese
Undergo a terrible metamorphosis,
Changing us into hideous monsters.
Who ever thought one lifeless notice,
Born from a kind people in a time of crisis,
Could cause such a chasm between Americans?
One country of people,
Torn asunder by a few men, and a leaf of paper.
Should I acquiesce, or dare I denounce it?

I watch in horror as my father,
Burns everything that is Japanese.
As the fire flickers,
My heart burns,
But how can I challenge,
For if I try,
The paper will win.

Brian Lund, 9th grade
Newport High School, Bellevue, Washington

Kryptonite and Fire

Kryptonite and fire
burning through
the pretty snowflakes
melting a hole
where petals surround
the stone
a light breeze
carries the spirit
where the sun shines above
sending rays for warmth
so the flowers bloom
for attraction
bringing others
near
while more daisies pop up
through the hot sand
where the blue hits
the grains
which have prints
that vanish
throughout the night
until new ones
are planted

Kimberly Wilson, 12th grade
Haddonfield Memorial High School
Haddonfield, New Jersey

Graveyard beside Whitesville Road

In March, snorting bulldozers and lumber cutters ripped out
slash pines, kudzu, Virginia creeper, and prickly briars,
piled them on mud-colored trucks and hauled them away.

In April, earth-eating, grunting monsters tore into the land
    making great hills one day,
        long orange ridges with shadowy valleys of death the next.
Better than ninety acres wedged between the bypass and
    Interstate
        just behind the new Publix, Big B Drugs and TCBY.

Now it's May. For sale signs are up.
In a forgotten parcel, seventeen gravestones huddle in weeds,
a twenty-by-forty-foot plot behind a rusted wrought iron fence
someone put there to mark the place.
Traffic whirls by these seventeen
    Fortsons, Blanchards, and Johnsons,
        side by side like rectangular blocks
        in a kindergarten.

It's an ugly garden of graves
beside an uglier tract where Cineplex
and Megatown will grow before long.
All that remains of a farm—
    a home where Johnsons,
    Blanchards and Fortsons
    lived un-airconditioned lives,
        fields where fat black and white cattle ate sweet grass,
        a murky gully where blotchy pigs rooted for rotten
        crabapples,

woods deep with sweet gum, and water oak, and
white pine,
    where children played hide-and-seek,
    and mumbledepeg,
    where Ivy Blanchard was kissed by a stranger
    in broad daylight,
    and Jack Fortson's hound ran off one night
    and was never seen again.

James Brewbaker
Flint River Review (1997)

Jim Brewbaker's Explanation of "Graveyard beside Whitesville Road"

Columbus, Georgia, has undergone much growth in the past few years. When I saw this sad little graveyard being overwhelmed by "progress" in the form of a new mall, it saddened me. I made a point one day of stopping there and taking pictures of the graves.

    The poem is simultaneously descriptive of what I saw that day and speculative. What was life like for those who had lived on that farm fifty or one hundred years ago? How did they pass their days, their "un-airconditioned lives"? In my mind's eye, I could see that tract in earlier, simpler times.

The Hill

On the hill, on the hill
The old house stands
The cold wind blows
The cows gaze
The children find sanctuary
The grandparents nap

On the hill, yes on the hill
Where a girl once lived
A house once stood
The wind no longer blows
The cows have also gone

On the hill, no longer a hill
Surrounded by yellow tape
Machines busily work
And the old children
Now grandparents weep
On the old hill

Robert Renshaw, 7th grade
Redlands Middle School
Grand Junction, Colorado

Sonnet for the Heart

My mind can learn the clear, blunt facts
Of violence, poverty, and pain
In history books and newsbreak stats
I hear again their icy names
But the paper's hard, black print
My grasping heart won't understand
It can't conceive the sword blade's glint

Or hold inside each dying man
Upon the field a thousand scream
Ten thousand fall, the mind will cope
My heart cries out, "Another dream,
Another love, another hope . . . "
Stiff upon a bloody stain
Another heart like mine is slain.

Hannah Fries, 10th grade
Bow High School, Bow, New Hampshire

Unchained

Tell freedom that I can wait no more
My body is tired and weak
With the pain of chains that cling to
My arms and legs and drag behind me
On the floors
Tell freedom that I starve for food
I don't get much and I need water
That overflows my cup
Tell freedom that there is no morn
Where I'll hear the sounds of birds singing
And children in a garden daily cared for
Tell freedom I had hope and pride in the things I
Worked for
But yesterday is over and I walk chained
No more

Ayesha Taylor, 12th grade
Onalaska High School, Onalaska, Washington

Pictures of the World
October 24, 1983
6:30 A.M.

Bearers cross the screen
with olive-green body bags.
Torches burn through spaghettied steel.
Like raccoons in garbage,
masked Marines forage for bodies.
A soldier kneels beside an arm.
The fingers move.

Cut to Peter Jennings:
"Records of the dead are lost,"

to Camp LeJeune, Georgia:
fresh troops at "fever-pitch"
wrestle duffle bags,

to Jane Pauley
asking an old, black woman
"How do you feel, not knowing
if your son is alive or dead?"

Kay Meier
English Journal (February 1990)

CHAPTER ELEVEN

The Future: Goals and Dreams

A mid the welter of factors—socioeconomic, psychological, political, cultural, and otherwise—that shape an individual's life, one thing that sometimes helps set apart happy, successful individuals, whether teachers or test pilots or teenagers, from those who drift or just get by is the ability to set goals, to dream purposefully about what the future will bring, and to take steps today to affect what tomorrow will be. Though this may differ in some cultures, most American adolescents have a strong sense of the future, a combination of excitement and dread, a need to try on new responsibilities combined with a need for the relative certainty of childhood. Adolescents need to plan for life after high school, whether that means further education or work.

Today's young people need opportunities—both in English classrooms and elsewhere—to consider what, in fact, "success" means. Does it come through career and financial gain? Through serving others? Through relationships and happy family life? Those who study Americans born between 1981 and 1987—the twenty-two million teenagers at the turn of the twenty-first century—report that today's middle schoolers and high schoolers are both optimistic and ambitious. Many of them expect to go to college, expect to be professionals, and expect to live fulfilling lives as adults—but not necessarily through work. This, some suggest, may be why nearly half are involved in volunteer activity at least monthly (Begley, 2000, p. 55).

Literature would be far less interesting were it not for young characters who set goals and work to achieve them. In earlier generations, Americans read of poor but determined Ragged Dick in a series of Horatio Alger novels that affirmed the "rags to riches" theme—that is, the idea that hard work and thrift will bring one tangible rewards. Jeffrey Decker's nonfiction *Made in*

America: Self-Styled Success from Horatio Alger to Oprah Winfrey, uses analysis of autobiographical statements from Andrew Carnegie to Oprah Winfrey to explore the link between self making and nation building; it also discusses origins of the "American dream."

In Louisa May Alcott's *Little Women*, Jo knows she wanted to be a writer, and she takes risks to reach her goal. Margaret Walker's *Jubilee*, called by some "the African American *Gone with the Wind*," focuses on Vyry, a freed slave whose tenacity keeps her family together and helps them build for the future.

The process of setting goals and forming plans to reach those goals also brings to mind numerous inspiring nonfiction narratives. Richard Wright's *Black Boy* and Gordon Parks's *A Choice of Weapons* relate the experiences of African Americans who succeed against great odds in a racist society. Among other works, teachers will find that many adolescents enjoy Homer Hickam's *Rocket Boys* (as well as Joe Johnston's 1999 film version, *October Sky*), which depicts Hickam's adolescence in a dying West Virginia mining town, where he negotiates family tensions and beats the odds to build a rocket and win a gold medal in the 1960 National Science Fair; he later became a NASA engineer. Many adolescents also enjoy Richard Rodriguez's *Hunger of Memory: The Education of Richard Rodriguez*; the author is a Hispanic American who grew to maturity in Southern California.

Recent adolescent literature offers many instances of young characters with big goals and dreams. Gary Soto's *Jesse* depicts Latino brothers toiling as agricultural workers, first in order to survive, then to plan for a better future. Lyddie, in Katherine Paterson's novel of the same name, spends endless hours in a New England textile mill because she wants to better herself through education. A similar ambition energizes LaVaughn in Virginia Euwer Wolff's *Make Lemonade,* a novel we have discussed in an earlier chapter. LaVaughn takes on an after-school job only after she convinces her mother that preparing for college will remain her first priority.

In other recent works, goals and dreams may be short-term rather than lifelong. In Mary Ann McGuigan's *Cloud Dancer,* for instance, Eileen displays great tenacity in finding money to buy a guitar and pay for lessons to help her speech-impaired younger brother. In *Dean Duffy,* Randy Powell tells the story of an injured adolescent baseball player who faces hard choices about setting new, realistic priorities for education after graduation. Finally, in Jean Thesman's *Cattail Moon,* fifteen-year-old Julia and her mother clash over conflicting goals: Julia has a passion for classical music, but her mother wants her to be a cheerleader.

The poets whose work is included in this chapter may describe life as a journey (Raymond Walters's "Scenic Route" and Shannon Tharp's "Night"), as a creative act (Toni Conley's "Science Project"), or as a natural paradise (Brittany Dixon's "Welcome"). Some, like Kate Slaga ("In My Head Are Dreams") sense a tension between doing what is expected by others and doing what is in one's heart. And still others (Camille Balaban's "a morning like this") are saddened to recall young people who, because of death, no longer have dreams. Jennifer Pattinson, in referring to herself and others as "keepers of the sky," captures in her poem "Sunset" the essential optimism that we find ourselves associating with Generation Next.

Reminiscences

Jim: I wasn't particularly goal-oriented as a teenager. At least that's how I remember it. By high school my life centered on music. Before long it was music and girls, more or less in that order.

Going to college was a given. My parents were both college educated, and I knew I'd enroll at the University of Virginia sooner or later. I couldn't imagine joining the army or going to work. But "going to college" was an abstraction to me. It wasn't linked to a life plan, and I suspect that's the way it is for most kids today. It certainly wasn't linked to hard work. Academics had always come easily for me. I assumed (incorrectly) that the same would be true in college as well.

Even my father's unexpected death the day before my nineteenth birthday didn't make me start thinking clearly about a future. If anything it set me back, because my father was my hero as a younger teen. I was a bit lost. Little did I know then that I'd be a married man and a father within three years. That made me grow up fast, whether I wanted to or not.

Dawnelle: For as long as I can remember, I've been a goal-oriented dreamer. Whether it was landing an A on a challenging pre-calculus test or subtly wooing the affections of that cute, intelligent boy in my seventh-grade science class, I've been clear about what I've wanted and gone for it—sometimes with gusto, other times with trepidation. My biggest test of commitment came during my eleventh-grade year. It was the first grading period, and I was failing chemistry. I had never failed anything before, and I admired my chemistry teacher, so I imposed upon myself a double incentive to do well. I studied harder than I ever had and steadily brought up my grade.

A pivotal point in my educational journey came when I decided to take on an unassigned multistep "challenge problem" in the back of our textbook. I worked on this—mostly through trial and error—for literally hours. When I finally solved it, I experienced an overwhelming sense of freedom and accomplishment! I had conquered the impossible on my own and had done it by allowing myself to try new paths, almost all of which were in the realm of the unknown to me. This brings to mind a life lesson I continue to learn: When I keep in full view a larger picture of where I'm headed, I can go powerfully for what I want; I limit myself only when I won't let go of what I know in order to pursue new avenues and opportunities.

References

Alcott, L. M. (1983). *Little women.* Los Angeles: Price Stern Sloan. (Original work published 1868, 1869)

Alger, H., Jr. (1998). *Ragged Dick and Mark the match boy (works of Horatio Alger Jr.).* New York: Simon & Schuster. (Original work published 1868)

Begley, S. (2000, May 8). A world of their own. *Newsweek, 135,* 53–56.

Decker, J. (1997). *Made in America: Self-styled success from Horatio Alger to Oprah Winfrey.* Minneapolis: University of Minnesota Press.

Hickam, H. (1998). *Rocket boys: A memoir.* New York: Delacorte.

Johnston, J. (Director), & Colick, L. (Writer). 1999. *October Sky.* Universal Pictures.

McGuigan, M. A. (1994). *Cloud dancer.* New York: Scribner's/Macmillan.

Parks, G. (1966). *A choice of weapons.* St. Paul: Minnesota Historical Society Press.

Paterson, K. (1991). *Lyddie.* New York: Lodestar Books.

Powell, R. (1995). *Dean Duffy.* New York: Farrar, Straus and Giroux.

Rodriguez, R. (1983). *Hunger of memory: The education of Richard Rodriguez: An autobiography.* New York: Bantam. (Original work published 1981)

Soto, G. (1994). *Jesse.* New York: Harcourt Brace.

Thesman, J. (1994). *Cattail moon.* Boston: Houghton Mifflin.

Walker, M. (1999). *Jubilee.* Boston: Houghton Mifflin. (Original work published 1966)

Wolff, V. E. (1993). *Make lemonade.* New York: H. Holt.

Wright, R. (1998). *Black boy.* New York: HarperPerennial. (Original work published 1945)

Night

Night.
The darkness and the shadows,
The fear and intensity.
It's my time to dream
About dreams to come,
Dreams that are,
Dreams that were and will never be.
A time to avoid
Uncomfortable situations
With sleep.
A time to drift over a
Sea of tranquil thoughts,
Without knowing which
Direction I am traveling.
I hear nothing,
For it is all mine,
That mood I like to call peacefulness.
All is calm
Deep within my slumber,
And I am alone.

Shannon Tharp, 9th grade
Twin Spruce Junior High School
Gillette, Wyoming

barefoot

amber toes with bleached nail crescents
dangle into cool water,
dipping into memories of burning summer sands and rain-
     softened grasses
like clear lake bottoms;
souls remember.

crisp mornings will follow.
one cannot remain barefoot.

unlike blankets which can be cast off,
work shoes harness in earnest:
straps chafe,
laces pinch,
heels throw us forward into the day.

contained and restrained,
we walk a straight path,
run the good race,
no longer naked beneath summer cottons.

only in summer
we dance.

Ann Rousseau
English Journal (April 1992)

Scenic Route

Bypassed by time and the interstate
the scenic route
conquers the landscape.
The original mile markers count down
to towns that no longer exist.
The sun low on the horizon
blends with the reds and oranges
of early autumn.
The scenic roads are being
obliterated by the
very growth
they created.
Barns rise darkly
casting shadows over fields
no longer farmed.
An abandoned Studebaker
and an International pickup
marvel over the dramatic sky
waiting for winter
in the encroaching forest.
The scenic road
is a good place to hide
from the modern world.
Driving along feeling
every bump under the wheels
and smelling the flowers among the weeds.
Tasting the sweet
blackberries growing
wild on the roadside.
Alone on a hill
a rusty windmill squeaks
as it spins in
the cool breeze.
A road is only pavement,
but a scenic road
is a time machine.
A metal sign in the middle
of the pavement

declares "ROAD ENDS".
Many travelers never get
to the end of the route.
Nothing wrong
with that. The most rewarding
dreams are not always
found at the end
of the road.

Raymond Walters, 11th grade
Clarkston High School, Clarkston, Michigan

In My Head Are Dreams

I always was a good little girl,
did what my mama told me,
when she told me.
Never once did I complain,
I swallow it all,
pushing it deeper.
Down, down, down.
Down to a place where right is wrong
and wrong is right.
A place where I wonder if
my actions are right,
because all the good leaves me feeling wrong
and all the right makes me crazy in the head.
And in my head are dreams,
dreams of wild nights and unspoken desires.
But I always wake
with tears on my cheeks
and the "right" thing
glaring me in the face.
One of these days
I might just become crazy enough
to glare back.

Kate Slaga, 10th grade
East High School, Denver, Colorado

Welcome

Welcome to my paradise where the flowers grow.
And in the afternoon, you can feel the sun's warm glow.

Welcome to my shining sea where the waters shimmer,
And on the beach, I sit and watch the waves as they glimmer.

Welcome to my windy forest where the flowers sigh,
Underneath the pale new moon
Which lights up the nighttime sky.

Welcome to my snowy mountains,
Where love shines like a golden ray,
And the music from my heart greets the brand new day.

Welcome to my misty meadows where nearby silent waters run,
There, the dew softly touches the flowers
Sparkling in the sun.

Welcome to the world I see when I close my eyes,
For if you imagine hard enough
There your sun will set and rise.

The world is perfect in my heart,
Filled with joy and love.

Its never-ending beauty is a gift
From up above.

If you hurt inside yourself,
And if you ever do,
Remember that my paradise
Is a place where dreams come true.

Brittany Dixon, 8th grade
Lee County Middle School, Leesburg, Georgia

Metaphor Poem

Life is a mountain-climbing expedition.
Most of it is spent taking lessons,
strapping on harnesses,
and checking safety gear.
Precious hours are spent preparing for the worst,
instead of planning for the best.
Few ever dare to grab hold of a rock,
plant their feet,
and climb toward destiny.

Caroline Glazenburg, 11th grade
Salmon Arm Senior Secondary School
Salmon Arm, British Columbia

Library of Life

Life is a mystery novel
With few clues on the cover.
Pay attention to the details,
They may reveal answers
To the future.
Insignificant characters may reappear
At unexpected times,
With momentous importance.
Some lives are short stories,
All too sad and brief;
Others are prolonged epics,
Wearing and exhausting to the end.
We find ourselves trying to follow the footsteps
Of fictional heroes.

Sheena Haines, 11th grade
Salmon Arm Senior Secondary School
Salmon Arm, British Columbia

The Unexpected

My mother answers the phone
late at night.
I listen to every word she says,
wait for her to hang up,
see the tears in her eyes,
hear the disappointment in her voice,
watch her head drop,
hear the dreadful news,
ask how this could happen,
wonder what the future holds,
hope for the best.

We never expect it,
but unwelcomed news does and will arrive
when we least expect it.
That one call or knock will
invade our peaceful existence.
Still, whatever the trouble,
we must look to the future,
pray for an answer,
and keep faith.
That is the only way we'll see
the light through the darkest times.

Casey Jo Humphreys, 10th grade
Hickman County High School
Clinton, Kentucky

a morning like this

if there can be a morning like this
when I sip coffee
with my nose inches from
a branch of lilac
sitting carelessly in an old ice bucket
on the kitchen table

and if the lavender scent
can distract me from the morning news
long enough for me to wonder
how those tiny flowerets
ever knew enough to bunch together
on a tough branch surrounded by
bright green leaves almost large enough
to overpower their fragrance

then, I guess I will live
beyond the glaring headlines
which tell of a full school bus
smashing into a car
containing five other students
from the same school
killing one young girl
who sat next to the driver

and, though lilacs won't bring back life
or ease the pain of the bus driver
a woman, who, only last year
buried her teenaged son
a boy who had chosen not to live
these purple buds
that open suddenly into lacey trumpets
soften, for me, the memory of that same boy
sitting in my class
taunting me with his impish ways
leaving me to wonder forever
why his days were so heavy
when, if he had looked, he might have seen
lilacs in bloom, robins in a green field
and the fact that tentative mornings
always offer enough possibility
to help us walk gently
through another day.

Camille Balaban
English Journal (January 1992)

Science Project

She rolls globes in her hands,
smears fingerpaints on styrofoam planets,
First the sun, screaming yellow,
bruised with bright spots and plagues;
then Earth, blue-green swirling
under clouds thumb-pressed;
battered Mercury scarred by fingernails;
Venus, tongue pink; Mars, ruling red;
bulging Jupiter, its hurricane eye
bloodshot, brooding;
gold Saturn crowned with cardboard
rainbow tinges, the Twins;
Uranus, methane green;
Neptune, the blue of virgins;
and Pluto, priest's purple rolled in glitter;
each speared with a popsicle stick,
axis stuck in a giftbox
covered with black construction paper
chalked with stars. my daughter's eyes
are hard and bright, wild with creating
her hair slipping from its band
spills around her face
smeared with primary colors.
A universe spins in our kitchen.
Each world in place, she goes to bed.
It spins while we are sleeping;
it spins silently not to wake us.

Toni Conley
English Journal (March 1992)

Learning to Ride

We are both nervous;
  he, astride the bike,
  I, standing beside him,
  the training wheels unbolted
  and discarded like crutches
  after a miraculous cure.

We have done this now
  for several days, aiming down
  the sidewalk, ready to launch
  ourselves like rockets;
  I, in spirit and in memory,
  he, in anticipation.

We work together again.
  I push, he pedals, and then he moves away
  from me, wobbly-wheeled,
  our breaths collectively caught
  in our throats, hoping that this time will be the charm.

He makes the magic, defies gravity,
  and forgetting the falls that hurt us both
  he gains speed and confidence,
  pumping his legs, swelling my heart,
  even as he flies from me
  down the walk and around the corner.

I stand alone and proud, calling after him,
  but sensing that my boy is disappearing,
  is speeding away buoyed by his new-found
    skill.
  He will return this time, I know:
  the block we live on is small. But
  a wider world is waiting.

Jerrol Leitner
English Journal (October 1993)

She Sat by the Water

She sat by the water.
Waiting.
Waiting like a lonely flower on a windless day.
Waiting and watching as the walls of her world fell around her.
They crumbled down.
Down to the floor.
Leaving her exposed and yearning for comfort.
Soon, as if in a dream, her petals began to drift away.
A new adventure was unraveling before her.
She was frightened.
She would have to face this one alone.
Because without her colorful mask,
She had no where to hide.
Finally . . .
    She took a breath . . .
        Dried her eyes . . .
            And walked forward.
She realized what she had to do.
She was ready to face the world.

Jillian Balser, 11th grade
Holy Name Central Catholic Junior/Senior High School
Worcester, Massachusetts

Keeping His Head
For Jacob

People were always telling him:

"Get your head out of the clouds!"

as if the clouds were a bad place for his head to be.
he liked having it there
where his thoughts could bump into each other
and even rain when they got too heavy.
He could think of worse places . . .
But in the day-to-day of things
it didn't work out to be so distant, so dreamy,

s o   s p a c e d   o u t.

His teachers and parents were
happier if he kept his head in mathematics
and current events. They didn't know
how hard it was, especially on clear days
when he could see the white shapes outside his
window—

Cumuli, nimbi, strati
aye, aye, aye
it made him dizzy.

That's why he dyed his hair blue, you see:
to keep the sky nearby
while he was required to keep his head
on earth.

Kathi Appelt
Just People and Other Poems for Young Readers
& Paper/Pen/Poem: A Young Writer's Way to Begin

Sunset

the clouds
reflect
the beauty of the nighttime
sky
unseen by most
except for us
the keepers of the sky

Jennifer Pattinson, 11th grade
Merritt Secondary School
Merritt, British Columbia

Book Resources for Using and Teaching Poetry

Carey, Michael A. *Poetry: Starting from Scratch: A Two Week Lesson Plan for Teaching Poetry Writing*. Lincoln, NE: Foundation Books, 1989. ISBN 0-934988-17-X.

"I'll show you how to get love into writing." So croons writer-poet Michael Carey in this slim volume built around a two-week plan for bringing just about everyone (kids, adults, prison inmates) to poetry. Written in an emphatic, strong voice, *Starting from Scratch* shows how writers and poets use all six senses, including "what you feel in your heart."

Collom, Jack. *Moving Windows: Evaluating the Poetry Children Write*. New York: Teachers & Writers Collaborative, 1985. ISBN 0-915924-55-2.

According to Jack Collom, children tend to write works that contain wonderful flashes of poetry. On the other hand, they have little appetite for revision, and their works are often "lifelessly conventional or generalized." Collom worked from 1980 to 1985 with New York City children in grades 4 to 8 to develop this warmhearted how-to book.

Collom, Jack, and Sheryl Noethe. *Poetry Everywhere: Teaching Poetry Writing in School and in the Community*. New York: Teachers & Writers Collaborative, 1994. ISBN 0-915924-98-6.

Sheryl Noethe writes, "When I read a poem to the class I read it as if it were the most important and only poem in the world." She and Jack Collom of *Moving Windows* used their stint as poets-in-residence in rural Montana to stimulate an entire community to the joys of poetry. This book is simultaneously practical and moving.

Copeland, Jeffrey S. *Speaking of Poets: Interviews with Poets Who Write for Children and Young Adults*. Urbana, IL: National Council of Teachers of English, 1993. ISBN 0-8141-4622-8.

This valuable reference for both teachers and students highlights sixteen poets (among them Gary Soto, Arnold Adoff, and Eve Merriam) in five- to six-page interviews. Copeland draws out his subjects through questions eliciting biographical information of interest to young people, as well as comments on how they came to write poetry and how they hope young people will respond to their work.

Denman, Gregory A. *When You've Made It Your Own: Teaching Poetry to Young People.* Portsmouth, NH: Heinemann, 1988. ISBN 0-435-08462-3.

In his introduction to this engaging work, Bill Martin calls Gregory Denman "Johnny Poemseeder," an apt description. Denman, baffled by the ignorance of many teachers about poetry, explains how elementary teachers can bring poetry to life. The volume is organized into two sections: Understanding Poetry (purpose, nature, and elements) and Teaching Poetry (problems, reading, writing).

Dias, Patrick X. *Reading and Responding to Poetry: Patterns in the Process.* Portsmouth, NH: Boynton/Cook, 1996. ISBN 0-86709-372-2.

Dias's work is a research report grounded in response theory. Teachers," he observes, ". . . walk an uneasy tightrope between a commonplace misrepresentation of response-centered teaching as 'a poem or story is *whatever* you want it to mean' and the widely held notion that meaning is resident entirely in the text. . . ." An important contribution to our understanding of what happens when teachers and kids meet text.

Duke, Charles R., and Sally A. Jacobsen (eds.). *Poets' Perspectives: Reading, Writing, and Teaching Poetry.* Portsmouth, NH: Boynton/Cook, 1992. ISBN 0-86709-304-8.

Recognizing a "need for broader perspectives," the editors of this collection of twenty-four essays by poets, teacher-poets, and teachers offer ideas to make poetry study and writing in the classroom more pleasant and meaningful. Among the highlights are Tom Liner's "The Outlaws . . . and Jonathan Smiling" and Marie Wilson-Nelson's "Faded Blue Jeans and Wool Turtlenecks: How One Writer Learned to Trust Poetry to Teach Itself."

Dunning, Stephen, and William Stafford. *Getting the Knack: 20 Poetry Writing Exercises 20.* Urbana, IL: National Council of Teachers of English, 1992. ISBN 0-8141-1848-8.

This NCTE bestseller may be the ultimate gimmick book on how to help learners (grade 6 through adult) create satisfying, even powerful, poetry. In fact, though Dunning and the late William Stafford describe their well-written, carefully sequenced chapters as gimmicks, one soon grasps that they have something bigger and better in mind.

Fagin, Larry. *The List Poem: A Guide to Teaching & Writing Catalog Verse*. New York: Teachers & Writers Collaborative, 1991. ISBN 0-915924-37-4.

This is, in the vernacular, a "fun book." In it, Larry Fagin discusses how to help children write engaging catalog poems, and his ideas generalize to teaching poetry writing as a whole. He promotes "a sense of shared fun and excitement" and avoids grades, competition, and favoritism. His method is closely aligned with process theory.

Glover, Mary Kenner. *A Garden of Poets: Poetry Writing in the Elementary Classroom*. Urbana, IL: National Council of Teachers of English, 1999. ISBN 0-8141-1823-2.

A teacher and principal at Awakening Seed School (Arizona), of which she was cofounder, Glover argues for the importance of helping children write poetry that is integrated with their lives at home and in school. In his foreword, Donald Murray observes that Glover is simultaneously passionate and practical: "Mary Glover's garden works."

Grossman, Florence. *Getting from Here to There: Writing and Reading Poetry*. Montclair, NJ: Boynton/Cook, 1982. ISBN 0-86709-033-2.

Grossman offers "a way to get at your poems by using them as a springboard into the poems of others." The volume is organized around ten forms and topics: people, image, lists, sound/silence, dreams, and others. It may be used by individual students or small groups.

Grossman, Florence. *Listening to the Bells: Learning to Read Poetry by Writing Poetry*. Portsmouth, NH: Boynton/Cook, 1991. ISBN 0-86709-274-2.

Grossman's "hope is that this book will be a Saturday/Sunday experience in the everyday English classroom." She believes that autobiographical experience is the heart of poetry writing and (eventually) of poetry reading. Interesting chapters include "The Rooms We Live In/ The Rooms We Leave Behind" and "I Am Not Who You Think I Am."

Jago, Carol. *Nikki Giovanni in the Classroom.* Urbana, IL: National Council of Teachers of English, 1999. ISBN 0-8141-5212-0.

Teacher-writer Jago has contributed a very useful resource in this first volume in the NCTE High School Literature Series. Both teachers and students will find worthwhile primary and secondary materials for research on the popular poet—poems, analyses, interviews, and more.

Janeczko, Paul (ed.). *Poetspeak: In Their Work, about Their Work.* New York: Atheneum, 1983. ISBN: 0027477703.

Well known as an anthologist, Paul Janeczko offers here what may be the best resource for teachers who want their students to understand what poets have to say about their own work. Sixty-two modern poets (and more than twice that number of their poems) are featured.

Marzán, Julio (ed.). *Luna, Luna: Creative Writing Ideas from Spanish, Latin American, and Latino Literature.* New York: Teachers & Writers Collaborative, 1997. ISBN 0-915924-52-8.

Acknowledging Federico García Lorca, Pablo Neruda, and Gabriel García Márquez, Marzán promotes Spanish, Latin American, and Latino and Latina literature and its influence, though he insists that "the ethnic focus of this book is secondary." Especially appealing essays include Mark Statman's "Reading and Seeing: Teaching Bilingual Calligrams" and Carol Bearse's "Singing with the Words: Using Neruda and Lorca with Middle-School Students."

Michaels, Judith Rowe. *Risking Intensity: Reading and Writing Poetry with High School Students.* Urbana, IL: National Council of Teachers of English, 1999. ISBN 0-8141-4171-4.

Some who work with writing workshop speak of the need to "write naked"—that is, to bare oneself and one's experiences to achieve writing that is both honest and intense. This, among a series of well-delineated teaching strategies, is what Judith Michaels is getting at in a book that is simultaneously energizing and practical. A welcome addition to the professional library of teachers who take writing seriously.

Moon, Brian. *Studying Poetry.* NCTE Chalkface Series. Urbana, IL: National Council of Teachers of English, 2001. ISBN 0-8141-4850-6.

Moon attends to connections between poetry and experience even as he emphasizes analysis and inquiry in inviting students to explore poetry as a form of discourse governed by social and historical conventions. The book includes activities tied to reprinted poems from the fourteenth century to the present, step-by-step guidelines for writing about poetry, annotated examples of student writing, and sample teacher comments. Moon also offers accessible theoretical accounts of poetry ranging from Plato to poststructuralist and feminist critics.

Somers, Albert B. *Teaching Poetry in High School.* Urbana, IL: National Council of Teachers of English, 1999. ISBN 0-8141-5289-9.

In a book that is both practical and comprehensive, the author addresses everything from how to select poems for classroom use, to using poetry across the curriculum, to finding and publishing poems on the World Wide Web. What about rap? Somers provides reasonable and theoretically sound answers to this and other questions.

Thomas, Lorenzo (ed.). *Sing the Sun Up: Creative Writing Ideas from African American Literature.* New York: Teachers & Writers Collaborative, 1998. ISBN 0-915924-54-4.

Thomas argues that African American literature is too often taught for its sociological significance rather than as literature. This collection of essays, intended for secondary and college teachers of English, ranges from Renee-Noelle Felice's "'Knoxville, Tennessee': Using Nikki Giovanni's Poem" to Len Roberts's "First Line/Rhythm Poems: Taking Off from Langston Hughes."

Tsujimoto, Joseph I. *Teaching Poetry Writing to Adolescents.* Urbana, IL: National Council of Teachers of English, 1988. ISBN 0-8141-5226-0.

In introducing this powerful work, Charles Suhor notes that Joseph Tsujimoto is in the mainstream tradition of Kenneth Koch, Daniel Fader, and Ken Macrorie. One might add James Moffett and Carl Rogers. An eighth-grade teacher, Tsujimoto passionately describes how poetry writing is more than craft and understanding; it also taps into the soul of learning.

Wilson, Lorraine. *Write Me a Poem: Reading, Writing, and Performing Poetry.* Portsmouth, NH: Heinemann, 1994. ISBN 0-435-08823-8.

Grounded in whole language theory, Wilson's volume—published first in Australia—links poetry to a child's emerging language skills. She describes in practical terms how to move upper-elementary youngsters from rhyme to free verse. Her perspectives on performance poetry and reader's theater are especially valuable.

Annotated List of Recent English Journal *and* Voices from the Middle *Articles on Using and Teaching Poetry*

Anderson, Anne P. "Doing Poetry." *Voices from the Middle* 6.2 (December 1998): 28–36.

> Inspired by a Poetry Alive! workshop, Anderson introduced her eighth graders to poetry via performance. Using small groups to plan and practice, students then performed poems they chose. Through performance, the students connected with the poets' words and devices. Anderson's students developed an authentic hunger for poetry.

Barbieri, Maureen. "To Open Hearts." *Voices from the Middle* 5.1 (February 1998): 29–35.

> Barbieri passionately shares her view of why poetry is important. She emphasizes that poetry allows students and teachers to "take the moments in our lives . . . and find both beauty and significance there." Poetry, she believes, connects us to other people and helps us to really see what is around us. It enables us to "write our memories and relive our lives. . . . We write to understand."

Burk, David. "Teaching the Terrain of Poetry." *English Journal* 81.3 (March 1992): 26–31.

> Poetry, writes Burk, is "a terrain whose boundaries are forever in dispute." With this in mind, he provides four "truths" that students should know about writing poetry. These ideas are based on observations of what poets do; they are brief and to the point and provide guidance for students without obstructing their creative, original spirit.

Cordi, Kevin. "Poetry Aloud." *English Journal* 86.1 (January 1997): 99–101.

> Cordi evokes student excitement about poetry. Small groups pick a topic, then search for related poetry by poets great and small. They read and record on tape what they find and what they write on their own. Cordi says they should use music, sound effects, a poster, a commentary—"anything that would bring life to the tape." For two days, the class reveled in poetry and their own creativity.

Frazier, C. Hood, and Charlotte Wellen. "The Way In Is the Way Out: Poetry Writing in the Classroom." *Voices from the Middle* 5.1 (February 1998): 3–9.

> Believing that poetry writing is a "transforming act," Frazier and Wellen show how students may explore language, themselves, and the world beyond. They approach poetry in three ways: becoming comfortable with word and with language play, exploring different forms and functions of poetry, and writing poems from personal experiences in a workshop setting.

Gardoqui, Kate E. "Double-Dutch, Hopscotch, B-ball, and . . . Poetry! Using Children's Games to Create Performances of Rhythmic Poems." *Voices from the Middle* 6.2 (December 1998): 11–18.

> This eighth-grade teacher shares how—through games—she made writing and performing poetry a positive experience for her students. Her middle schoolers first learned about rhythmic poetry and the importance of rhythm. Her activities, making students comfortable and confident, built their excitement about performing, which, she notes, enables them to "own the poem."

Greenway, William. "Poems and Paintings: Shades of the Prison House." *English Journal* 85.3 (March 1996): 42–48.

> Greenway helps students "marry" poetry and paintings. Writing poems about works of art allows students to express personal interpretations of what they see. Thus, they gather from each other both what is universal and what is unique to personal experience. Greenway learned that writing about art engages students in deeper play with words. Though most appropriate for high school students, these strategies could benefit younger students as well.

Hobgood, Jayne M. "Finders Keepers: Owning the Reading They Do." *Voices from the Middle* 5.2 (April 1998): 26–33.

Hobgood wants students to own their reading, "so they can take from literature a deeply felt meaning for their own lives." For this reason, she prompts them to use their imagination, autonomy, and creativity. Students look at favorite passages, then at a particular word, which acts as a springboard for writing poetry. Thus they are able to use reading logs as a way to "find" poems in their own writing.

Jester, Judith. "Audience and Revision: Middle Schoolers *Slam* Poetry." *Voices from the Middle* 4.1 (February 1997): 43–46.

Jester puts herself in the shoes of her students. Not only does she write with them, she also reluctantly performed her work at monthly poetry slams. She then transplanted this idea into her classroom. She and another teacher staged a joint poetry reading competition through which students saw the value of an objective rating of their poems and were encouraged to read and write more.

King, Wendy. "Stealing a Piece of the World and Hiding it in Words." *Voices from the Middle* 4.1 (February 1997): 22–29.

In this enriching poetry unit for eighth grade, King exposed her students to various poetic forms. While immersed in reading poetry, they wrote their own poems. King used peer revision, and her students discovered that poems revised by classmates were much stronger. Along the way, they developed a knack for identifying poetic techniques. Through poetry, students could "tell who (they) are and explore what (they) don't know."

Lardner, Ted, Barbara Sones, and Mary E. Weems. "'Lessons Spaced by Heartbeats': Performance Poetry in a Ninth-Grade Classroom." *English Journal* 85.8 (December 1996): 60–65.

Lardner, Sones, and Weems share wonderful activities designed to spark creative writing as well as enable students to find poetry in their own lives. From their experiences with these strategies, students became excited about sharing and performing their work. Performance was essential because "in performance writers bring words to life."

Lockward, Diane. "Poets on Teaching Poetry." *English Journal* 83.5 (September 1994): 65–70.

Reaching out to teachers who feel unqualified to teach poetry, Lockward shares the views of several poets on how poetry should be taught. The poets (among them Marie Howe and Robert Kendall) recommend oral reading, opportunities to make connections between poems and experiences, freedom of interpretation, and, when writing poetry, free selection of topics.

Mitchell, Diana. "Putting Poetry in Its Place." *English Journal* 83.5 (September 1994): 78–80.

In detailing a dozen engaging strategies, Mitchell says that poetry should be all over the place if one is teaching high school English well. Rather than teaching a poetry unit, she prefers weaving poetry into the "fabric of the class." Her strategies are sound for both college prep and general English classes.

Perreault, George. "Writing from the Limbic Brain: A (Perhaps) Foolproof Way to Generate Student Poetry." *English Journal* 85.6 (October 1996): 103–104.

Though a simple idea, Perreault illustrates a unique activity to stimulate poetry writing. Students sample the smell of various spices and record what comes to mind, then write poems based on the things, people, places, or events that they recalled when smelling a particular spice. This activity sparks creativity and imagination and seems suitable for many age groups.

Ridolfi, Kerry. "Secret Places." *Voices from the Middle* 4.1 (February 1997): 38–42.

After teaching poetry, Ridolfi discovered that students will write when "they are challenged, yet feel comfortable and safe," and when they are moved. She exposed her students to a variety of poems as well as focusing on language and poetic devices. She encouraged students to write using other poems as models. She notes that students often wrote about dreams, hopes, and loneliness. Writing poetry enables them to open up the "secret places."

Robertson, Jackie. "Poetry in Science." *Voices from the Middle* 4.2 (April 1997): 7–10.

Robertson's seventh-grade science class did the impossible: to mix science and poetry. She shares how poetry lets students use their creativity while learning scientific concepts. Sensing that most students are intimidated by poetry, she helped them write group poems at first, then introduced the concepts of cells and similes. Eventually, students wrote poems about rainforests.

Thomas, P. L. "It Beckons, and It Baffles—": Resurrecting Emily Dickinson (and Poetry) in the Student-Centered Classroom." *English Journal* 87.3 (March 1998): 60–63.

Most young people do not enjoy the classics—even perennial teacher's favorite Emily Dickinson. Thomas proposes that "teachers must revitalize themselves as experts" and relates how he uses lyrics by the rock group REM to illustrate poetic techniques. By comparing Dickinson's poems with REM's lyrics, students better understand both. Useful in both middle school and high school, Thomas's strategy would also work with other classic literature.

Walsh, Christopher S. "PSL—Poetry as a Second Language: Breaking the Silence." *Voices from the Middle* 5.1 (February 1998): 20–26.

Walsh exposes ESL students to the English language through poetry. Realizing that his students have minimal exposure to English, he uses poetry as a way to help them connect emotionally with a new language. The students read poetry translated from their native language, as well as poetry in English, and they write poems in both languages. Though labeled "Limited English Proficient," Walsh's students learn how to reinvent their thoughts, feelings, and ideas in English.

Recommended Web Sites on Poetry in the Classroom

About (The Human Internet): Creative Writing for Teens (http://teenwriting.about.com/?once=true&)

A youth-centered site that encourages writing of all varieties, including poetry. Previously e-published poems and prose pieces are organized by theme. Their quality is predictably uneven. The site owner would, in addition, love to sell teens the latest products, but the pitch is generally unobtrusive.

Academy of American Poets (www.poets.org/index.cfm)

This is a truly rich site offering discussion lists, poetry sharing (and constructive critiquing), and—best of all—recordings of poets from Frost to Soto reading their work. One could get (happily) lost in this site. The Online Poetry Classroom Project, begun in 2000, is a resource valuable to both teachers and students.

Ask ERIC Lesson Plans (http://askeric.org/Virtual/lessons/)

Teachers who haven't visited this site are working with one hand tied behind their backs. A rich source of teaching ideas for all subject areas and grade levels, with poetry lessons that include Performance Poetry for Grades 7–12, Poetry Cubes, and Poetry Pals Using the Internet.

Syllaweb (http://www.tnellen.com/cybereng/log.html)

NCTE's Ted Nellen is a Web-based teacher extraordinaire. This site allows one to look over his shoulder (and his students' shoulders). Nellen features forty-five (count 'em!) projects and activities, from Aphorisms to Shakespeare to Zen Stories. Number 37 is Poetry. It and others are well worth sampling.

Poetry and the Computer (www.abcplace.com/poetry)

This is a user-friendly site for nonspecialist teachers (especially in grades 3-7) who want to emphasize poetry beyond their present practice. Anne Curtin provides classroom exercises that are easy to adopt and adapt, sensible advice from the Academy of American Poets, and poems by Maurice Sendak, Lee Bennett Hopkins, and others keyed to a school-year calendar.

Poetry Etc. (www.freeyellow.com/members/mrlatman/poetry.html)

Developed by Chicago English teacher Gary Latman for his students, this site is short on its own content but very long on links to poet sites (e.g., Gwendolyn Brooks, Charles Bukowski, Allen Ginsberg) and teen-oriented sites such as Youth Central, Writes of Passage, and KidPub, among others.

Poet's Corner (www.geocities.com/Athens/Acropolis/2012/poems/index.html)

This is a rich site on traditional poets (763 of them) and their work (6,533 poems). A subject index (sports, love, seasons, and so forth) can be particularly useful. It would be a major undertaking, but the site would be far better if it included more contemporary poets. Robert Frost? No problem. Randall Jarrell and Nikki Giovanni? Sorry.

Teachers & Writers Collaborative (http://www.twc.org/)

This nonprofit publisher of books for writers and teachers of writing (see our list of recommended books for several examples), has put together a solid Web site for writing and poetry enthusiasts. An active listserv on teaching poetry is a plus. One can download audio versions of various works read aloud by their creators.

Young Adult Literature: Middle & Secondary English-Language Arts (http://falcon.jmu.edu/~ramseyil/yalit.htm)

Inez Ramsey (from James Madison University) has put together a comprehensive resource for preservice teachers that will also prove invaluable to veterans. Poetry is *among* the many curriculum areas she features. Links to author Web sites are especially helpful.

List of Adolescent Poets' Hometowns, Schools, and Teachers

British Columbia

Chilliwack—Chilliwack Senior Secondary School
Rachel Devenish (12th grade)
Teacher: Gordon Yakimow

Merritt—Merritt Senior Secondary School
Jennifer Pattinson (11th grade)
Teacher: Laurie Barisoff

Salmon Arm—Salmon Arm Senior Secondary School
Caroline Glazenburg (11th grade)
Derik Gummesen (12th grade) (2 poems)
Sheena Haines (11th grade)
Teachers: Duncan Lowe and Karen Johanson

Vancouver—Little Flower Academy
Elena Rente (9th grade)
Teacher: Tracey Lee

California

San Jose—Lynbrook High School
Jaclyn Peterson (9th grade)
Teacher: Jennifer Goebel

Vacaville—Vaca Peña Middle School
Daniel Chavez (7th grade)
Teacher: Amy Labson

Colorado

Denver—East High School
Kate Slaga (10th grade)
Teacher: James Hobbs

Grand Junction—Redlands Middle School
Robert Renshaw (7th grade)
Tara Ritchie (7th grade) (2 poems)
Kellen Walter (7th grade)
Teacher: Vicki Stites

Connecticut

Brookfield—Brookfield High School
Jonathan Liebtag (10th grade)
Teacher: Patricia O'Connor

Greenwich—Greenwich Academy
Alexa Baz (10th grade)
Teacher: Marilyn Ebbitt

Greenwich—Brunswick School
David M. Darst Jr. (10th grade) (2 poems)
Teacher: Marilyn Ebbitt

Georgia

Columbus—Hardaway High School
Valerie Voter Bos (11th grade)
Teacher: Connie Ussery

Dalton—Southeast Whitfield High School
John Cameron (10th grade)
Joseph McGill (10th grade)
Brandy Ogle (11th grade)
Josh Robinson (11th grade)
Teacher: Sherrian Hall

Leesburg—Lee County Middle School
Brittany Dixon (8th grade)
Teacher: Dianne Lawton

Hamilton—Harris County Carver Middle School
Charity Koone (8th grade)
Devan Satterwhite (6th grade)
Teachers: Denise Crawford and Melanie Reiney

Hiawassee—Towns County High School
Tracy Thompson (9th grade)
Teacher: Melissa Patterson

Tyrone—Robert J. Burch Elementary School
Jessica Pratt (5th grade)
Teacher: Susan Mills

Idaho

Boise—Borah High School
Tiana Murphy (12th grade)
Teacher: Patricia Pierose

Rathdrum—Lakeland Junior High School
Crystal Gossard (8th grade)
Teacher: Dawn Mackesy

Illinois

Lake Forest—Lake Forest High School
Lucy Depree (12th grade)
Saritha Peruri (12th grade)
Margo Zuffante (9th grade)
Teacher: Margaret Forst

Orion—Orion High School
Corinne Lampe (12th grade)
Teacher: Karin Hamburg

Kentucky

Clinton—Hickman County High School
Casey Jo Humphreys (10th grade)
Teacher: Sherry Roberts

Warsaw—Gallatin High School
Mandy Glover (12th grade)
Teacher: Mrs. Howerton

Louisiana

Lafayette—Lafayette High School
Bonny Leah McDonald (12th grade)
Teacher: Melinda Mangham

New Orleans—St. Mary's Dominican High School
Courtney Bush (11th grade)
Myrna Enamorado (12th grade)
Teacher: Sara Lemle

Maryland

Berlin—Stephen Decatur Middle School
Lochanda Collick (7th grade)
Teacher: Janice A. Currence

Hyattsville—Hyattsville Middle School
Diana Levy (7th grade)
Nathan Marwell (7th grade)
Teacher: Patricia Bradford

Sandy Spring—Sherwood High School
Allison Stevens (9th grade)
Teacher: Peter Fallaw

Massachusetts

Worcester—Holy Name Central Catholic Junior/Senior High School
Jillian Balser (11th grade)

Michigan

Birmingham—Derby Middle School
Karlie Bryant (8th grade)
Teacher: Robert Smith

Clarkston—Clarkston High School
Jenny Davis (12th grade)
Susan Floyd (12th grade)
Katrina Gomez (9th grade)
Sarah Hool (12th grade)
Shannon Iezzi (12th grade)
Leah Lenk (12th grade)

Amy Licatovich (9th grade)
Laura Pope (12th grade)
Kristen Propst (12th grade)
Josh Sommers (12th grade)
Raymond Walters (11th grade)
Teachers: Tina Chambers and Alexis Pollock

Farm Hills—East Middle School
Tina Gupta (8th grade)
Teacher: Mary Ellen Thompson

Grand Ledge—Leon W. Hayes Middle School
Holly Bailey (8th grade)
Teacher: Diane Delaney

Monroe—St. Mary Catholic Central School
Jeremy Stoll (10th grade)
Teacher: Pamela Kobasic

Grosse Pointe—University Liggett School
Emily Tancer (6th grade)
Teacher: Karen Damphousse

Missouri

St. Louis—Parkway North High School
Andrea D. Firestone (12th grade)
Amanda Gagliardi (12th grade)
Tara Nicole Tonsor (12th grade)
Teacher: Melissa Lynn Pomerantz

Nebraska

Papillion—Papillion-LaVista High School
David Clark (12th grade) (2 poems)
Danielle Mangano (12th grade)
Heather Miser (12th grade)
Teacher: Margaret Shanahan

New Hampshire

Bow—Bow High School
Hannah Fries (10th grade)
Kaitlyn Gilles (10th grade)
Teacher: Denise Fournier

New Jersey

Flemington—Hunterdon Central Regional High School
Kristen Haver (12th grade)
Teacher: John Smith

Galloway—Arthur Rann Middle School
Emma Halpern (8th grade)
Teacher: Rosemary Fedon

Haddonfield—Haddonfield Memorial High School.
Kimberly Wilson (12th grade)
Teacher: Therese Willis

Howell—Howell Middle School
Maryann Matera (8th grade)
Teacher: Barbara Moss

Monmouth Junction—South Brunswick High School
Desirae Andrabovitch (9th grade)
Gina Marie Damiano (11th grade) (3 poems)
Tykeria T. Muhammad (9th grade)
Tiffany Brandy Trawick (12th grade)
Teacher: Joyce Lott

New Mexico

Roswell—Mesa Middle School
Shannon Barr (8th grade)
Teacher: Heidi Huckabee

New York

Delmar—Bethlehem Central Middle School
Andrew Shawhan (6th grade)
Teacher: Jody Rosenberger

Manhasset—Manhasset Middle School
Danielle Kaufman (7th grade)
Teacher: Leslie Skolnik

North Carolina

Barco—Currituck County High School
Jeremy Casey, 10th grade
Teacher: Valerie Person

Durham—North Carolina School of Science and Mathematics
Roodabeh Samimi (11th grade)
Teacher: Jane Shlensky

Ohio

Strongsville—Strongsville High School
Halle Butvin (11th grade)
Teacher: Linda Specht

Oklahoma

Norman—Norman High School
Lindsey J. Blackburn (12th grade) (3 poems)
Kristen MacGorman (10th grade)
Shannon Parkison (12th grade)
Teacher: Freeda Richardson

Pennsylvania

Lansdale—North Penn High School
Barry Floyd (11th grade)
Alison Faucher (12th grade)
Laura Beth Malick (12th grade)
Orion Nessly (12th grade)
Sarah Sando (12th grade)
Teacher: Kathie B. Walsh

Wayne—Radnor Middle School
John Steele (8th grade)
Teachers: William Byrne and Karyl Maenza

Texas

Houston—River Oaks Baptist School
Kelly Boss (6th grade)
Chris Gibbs (6th grade)
Jennifer Patterson (6th grade)
Ryan Starbird (6th grade)
Teacher: Michael Petrizzo

Magnolia—Magnolia High School
Pamela Buttner (10th grade)
Teacher: Leslie Walker

Utah

Smithfield—Sky View High School
Katie Moon (10th grade)
Teacher: Louise Letham

Virginia

Norfolk—Granby High School
Philip Odango (9th grade)
Teacher: Barbara S. Bowman

Washington

Bellevue—Newport High School
Brian Lund (9th grade)
Teacher: Nancy Potter

Onalaska—Onalaska High School
Ayesha Taylor (12th grade)
Teacher: Sue Roden

Spokane—Lewis & Clark High School
Adrian Pauw (12th grade)
Teacher: Sally Pfeifer

Wyoming

Gillette—Twin Spruce Junior High School
Shannon Tharp (9th grade)
Teacher: Joyce Keith

Editors

Photograph by L. B. Buker

James Brewbaker, now a teacher educator, taught English in grades 7–11 before completing graduate studies at the University of Virginia. He credits Guy Ellis and Bob Small, former editors of the *ALAN Review,* with sparking his love for YA literature. He has presented numerous papers on YA literature and contributed biographical-critical articles on Chris Lynch and Margaret Mitchell to *Writers for Young Adults* (1997, 2000). Active in NCTE circles, Brewbaker concluded a three-year term as chair of the Standing Committee on Teacher Preparation and Certification in late 1999. When asked by editor Leila Christenbury, he authored "On Tuesday Morning: The Case for *Standards for the English Language Arts*" for the January 1997 issue of *English Journal.* Brewbaker's passion for poetry is longstanding. Some years ago, he began writing with his students at Columbus State University. Gradually, he has sought larger audiences for his work and—less frequently than he would like—publishes a poem or two. He is professor of English education at Columbus State University.

Dawnelle J. Hyland has taught at Chewning Middle School (Durham, North Carolina) since 1996; currently, she teaches sixth-grade language arts and social studies on an inclusion team. She has also taught writing and social issues for summer programs serving at-risk students in Los Angeles and for the Duke Young Writers' Camp. A 1996 graduate of the University of North Carolina at Chapel Hill, she has begun the process of standing for licensure by the National Board for Professional Teaching Standards. Hyland enjoys both professional and local community service. She is a frequent presenter at NCTE conferences and serves on the National Advisory Board for the Student Coalition for Action in Literacy Education (SCALE), an organization that provides training and support for campus-based literacy programs. She also volunteers her time in building transformational training programs for youth and adults across the Southeast.

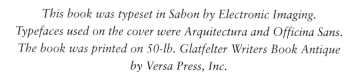

This book was typeset in Sabon by Electronic Imaging.
Typefaces used on the cover were Arquitectura and Officina Sans.
The book was printed on 50-lb. Glatfelter Writers Book Antique
by Versa Press, Inc.

1833